Understanding the SEED

McDougal & Associates
Servants of Christ and Stewards of the Mysteries of God

Understanding the SEED

A Divine Road Map for the Days Ahead

by

Pastor Peter Kange
Lady Jane Lowder
Dr. Harold McDougal
and
Prophetess Andy McDougal

Understanding the Seed
Copyright © 2014 by McDougal & Associates
ALL RIGHTS RESERVED under United States, Latin American, and International copyright conventions

Unless otherwise noted, all Scriptures references are from *The Holy Bible, King James Version* (public domain). References marked AMP are from *The Amplified Bible*, copyright © 1987 by the Zondervan Corporation and the Lockman Foundation, La Habra, California. References marked NKJV are from *The Holy Bible, New King James Version,* copyright © 1979, 1980, 1982, 1990 by Thomas Nelson, Inc., Nashville, Tennessee. References marked "NLT" are from *The New Living Translation of the Bible*, copyright © 1996 by Tyndale House Publishers, Inc., Wheaton, Illinois.

McDougal & Associates is dedicated to the spreading of the Gospel of the Lord Jesus Christ to as many people as possible in the shortest time possible.

Published by:

McDougal & Associates
18896 Greenwell Springs Road
Greenwell Springs, LA 70739
www.ThePublishedWord.com

ISBN: 978-1-940461-16-8

Printed on demand in the US, the UK, and Australia
For Worldwide Distribution

Contents

Introduction 7

1. Raising Up Those Dry Bones 9
2. Becoming Servant of All 43
3. Understanding the Seed, Part I 87
4. Obeying the Lord of the Harvest 121
5. Going to the Other Side 157
6. Understanding the Seed, Part II 193
7. Rebuilding a City 225
8. Activating the Seed 245
9. Understanding the Seed, Part III 269

Contact Information 307-309

INTRODUCTION
By Pastor Peter

In the early days of January of 2014, I was invited to be the evening speaker at the annual Ministers and Workers Convention at Calvary Campground in Ashland, Virginia. It was not my first time to speak there. I, my family, and my people love to go there as often as we can, and I had ministered there before. We love the place so much that we go as a church and help the camp staff to get ready each year for their summer camp season.

Calvary Campground is a blessing. People come there from all over the world to seek God. There is plenty of prayer, wonderful worship times, great freedom in the Spirit, and very challenging messages straight from the throne of God. The amazing thing is that the camp does not charge anything for food or accommodations, so anyone who is hungry for God can attend.

This camp and its activities are built on the great vision of a wonderful family of faith, the Heflins, and the current director, Pastor Jane Lowder, and her staff are all dedicated to carrying on the many wonderful traditions handed down to them and also to expanding that vision. No wonder the place is so blessed!

As wonderful as previous visits had been, this time proved to be something very special. Because the crowd was made up of those who had a calling and a burden to serve God, there was a special anointing present in every service, the praise and worship was especially blessed, and God began to speak to us in an unusual way from the very first service.

Not long into this great convention, it suddenly and powerfully dawned on me that what was being said was not just for 2014. God was laying a foundation for the future. I suggested that the messages being delivered be put into a book so that many more people could benefit from them. Fortunately one of the speakers, Dr. Harold McDougal, was a Christian book publisher, and he agreed to do just that. May multitudes be blessed and challenged by *Understanding the Seed*.

Pastor Peter Kange
Reaching the Nations Ministries International
Beltsville, Maryland

Chapter 1

Raising Up those Dry Bones
by Lady Jane Lowder

Are you ready to say, "I will go?" That's what God has said He wants to hear from us these days. Each of us must declare: "Wherever He leads, whatever He is speaking for me to do, I will arise and go forth in the name of the Lord." We can do that because He has conquered every foe by His name. In Him, we live, we move, and we have our being. In Him, we have a ministry. In Him, we can accomplish all things that He has called us to do. It is not by might, and not by power, but by His wonderful and glorious Spirit that He has invested within each of us.

Each one of us has an investment that comes with the Holy Spirit, and it is there to equip us and enable us to be ministers of the New Testament. Whether we understand it or not or can define it or not, each one of us has a ministry. It doesn't matter what walk of life we may have chosen, God has called each of us to minister for Him. He hasn't called us all to be pastors, and He hasn't called us all to be evangelists, but He has called every believer to be a minister of His wonderful Word and of His wonderful life in some way.

This is a great privilege, for we serve an awesome God. He is awesome in everything that He does, and He wants to touch each of us with His awesomeness so that we can go forth and bless others.

But ministry is not always easy and, at times, we become weary in our well-doing. We get tired. Sometimes this tiredness comes because we're not sure of the next step. Sometimes we actually don't even want to know the next step. This may be because we are not satisfied that we have finished the last step or finished it well enough. How can we move on, when we haven't done the job well up to now? If that is the case, then we need a miraculous touch from God to move us from one place to the next.

Get a Touch from Heaven

Some of you might be suffering in your body today, and, if so, you need a touch from Heaven because your body is important. It's not just a bunch of bones covered by meat. It's a house, and it houses the wonderful Holy Spirit, the third person of the Godhead. I believe He wants our house to be His house, and so He wants us to be healed, to be healthy, to be well, and He wants our bodies to look good.

God doesn't want us looking like we're half torn apart and barely able to move. He wants us to be full of excitement and joy and the strength that comes from Him. He wants you and I to be able to say, "For the joy that is set before us, we can follow on to know Him and to be and to do what He has called us to be and to do." If you have sickness or pain in your body or if you're feeling oppressed or depressed or just plain tired today, let God touch you so that you can enjoy this journey with our awesome God.

The most wonderful thing we can say about our awesome God is that He has chosen to live inside of us and to do wonderful things in us and through us. His will is to bring us forth into a new and wonderful place that He has prepared.

Mastering Our Feelings

If we Christians didn't have feelings, we could probably walk in victory a lot more than we do, but our feelings are given to us by God, and they're important. When it's cold outside, we feel it and bundle up more to protect us from the cold. If we feel hot, we fan ourselves or step into the shade or into an air-conditioned room. In the same way, we feel anger, disappointment, and discouragement, and all of these are natural feelings. The good news is that God has given us His wonderful Holy Spirit, His wonderful Word, and His wonderful personal promises to help us overcome what we may be feeling at the moment. He assures us, even before we enter into battle, that we are more than a conqueror (see Romans 8:37). He teaches us to call on Him for help in bringing into captivity our thoughts and corralling our feelings and imaginations (see 2 Corinthians 10:5). I have found that the best way to do this is to immediately rehearse what God has said on the subject.

When the enemy torments you, tell him, "I am God's favorite child, and I am anointed. My Father God has given me power over all the power of the enemy. Amen!" As we believe what God says and quote it back to Him, say it to ourselves, and use it to repel the enemy, something wonderful and powerful happens in us. God honors His promises every time.

Discovering the Dry Bones

Let's read a portion of Ezekiel 37, where the prophet recorded:

> *The hand of the Lord was upon me, and carried me out in the spirit of the Lord, and set me down in the midst of the valley which was full of bones, and caused me to pass by them round about: and, behold, there were very many in the open valley; and, lo, they were very dry.*
> *And he said unto me, Son of man, can these bones live? And I answered, O Lord God, thou knowest.*
>
> Ezekiel 37:1-3

Each of us, as ministers of Christ, must be willing for the Spirit to carry us where He wants to carry us, to show us what He wants to show us, and to use us in the way He wants to use us.

Like Ezekiel, when we are asked if something can be done, we can answer, "God knows." We don't know, but He always does. When He takes us someplace that we are unfamiliar with, that's okay, because He knows that place.

When He asks us to do something that is new to us, that's okay, because He knows how to do it. He can do all things, and nothing is impossible to Him. Therefore nothing is impossible for you or for me, as we believe Him to work through us.

God has wonderful places for us to go in the days ahead, places we've never gone before. And He has wonderful things for us to do that we've never done before. In one sense, this is exciting, but in another sense it can be terrifying. We may be excited until we get there and face the situation. But then, as we realize that we are not able to accomplish the assigned feat in ourselves, we sometimes actually get scared.

There may well be some difficulties to face along the way before we ever get to the appropriate place, but there is nothing that we will encounter that is too difficult for God. There is no place too hot for God and no place too cold for Him either. As we walk with Him, He will enable us to do what He has called us to do.

What God has called you to do and what He has called another person to do are probably two very different things. The important thing is to find His purpose for you and then allow Him to get glory from your life as you walk toward the goal or the finish line of what He has given you to do.

Ezekiel Welcomed the Hand of the Lord

Ezekiel was a prophetic person. He welcomed the hand of the Lord to be upon him, and he allowed himself to be carried out in the Spirit. Oh, that God's hand would be upon each of us these days in a greater measure and that He would carry us out by His Spirit into a place where we have not yet been and let us see things pertaining to our glorious future. If we are willing, God will sometimes show us the future in great detail.

Are you willing? Tell Him, "Show me, Lord!" All that happened to Ezekiel came because he welcomed the hand of the Lord to be upon him and the Spirit of the Lord to carry him out.

The things we see in the Spirit are not imaginary. They are life-changing. They bring us into new dimensions. They bring a new joy and a new strength to our lives. They cause us to want to arise and go forth in the name of the Lord.

My Vision of Jesus Coming

When I first came into knowing the Lord and understanding a little about visions, God showed me a wonderful vision of His Son Jesus. I saw Jesus coming down on a cloud, and it was so wonderful, so real, and so powerful that I thought He was coming right then. If you had told me that it would be nearly forty years later and He still hadn't come, I would have called you a liar. It was just that real. I wanted to go ring every doorbell and knock on every door and tell the people, "Jesus is coming." That sensation is still real today. He is still on His way, and His coming is now nearer than it was then.

I was so caught up with that vision that when I was outdoors, I would sometimes just stand and look at the sky, trying to see Jesus. People would stop and ask, "What are you looking at?"

I would say, "Jesus is coming." The vision was just that real in my heart, and I believe we still need a vision like that, something that will set us on fire, something that will keep us moving forward toward the next level in God. A vision like that will keep you alive in Him.

He is coming, but I can't say when. I thought it would happen in 1976, and here we are so many years later, and He hasn't come yet. That vision, however, is just as real today, and the excitement of it is still there. Jesus is coming, and He's coming for you and for me.

There are yet many who don't know Him, that have not met Him, that have yet to call upon His name. Thank God that He has you and me. Now we are obligated to show the way to those who have not yet heard.

My First Experiences at Camp

I arrived at Calvary Campground in Ashland, Virginia, in June of 1976, just fourteen days before the summer camp season was to begin. I went into the dining hall, and it was packed full of furniture and mattresses. There were just a few tables up for the camp staff to eat on, and there were some freezers along the back wall (they were all empty). In the course of our work, one of the sisters working back in the kitchen asked if she could pray for me. Of course, I said yes. She laid hands on me, and during her ministry, she said these words: "The book of Ezekiel is going to become very real to you." I was immediately carried out in the Spirit and saw the vision of Jesus again. He was coming, riding down on that cloud.

Inside I was saying, "Come, Lord Jesus! Come, Lord Jesus!"

Then the vision changed, and I saw many people and they were of all different colors. There were millions of them, and I began to cry out, sobbing, "Please, Jesus, don't come yet. Please, Jesus, don't come yet. Give me an opportunity to go and tell these people about You." In this way, He placed in my heart a desire to go and tell those who have not heard about Jesus and His coming, about His cross, about His love that had come into my life and into my spirit. I have never been the same since.

God Is Calling Us All

God is calling us all to go for Him. We cannot sincerely answer this call, however, unless and until He does something dramatic in our lives, showing us something that excites us and makes us want to arise and go wherever He wants to send us.

What He is asking for is more than just saying the words. We must say them with joy. If you just say words from your mind, you'll never really go. You have to say them from your spirit. The desire to go must be placed within you, so that from within, you cry out, "Here am I, Lord, send me." When it happens that way, you *will* go. If such a decision comes from the mind, it is easy later to change your mind and take another course. If it comes from your spirit, you will not rest until you have obeyed.

A Valley Was Full of Dry Bones

Suddenly Ezekiel saw something that greatly impacted his life. A valley was full of dry bones. This happened because he was open to being moved by the Spirit, and what he saw that day got inside of him and changed him forever.

Some would have rejected such a scene as being from the devil. Would God show you a place full of dead bones? That could not have been a pleasant scene, and many of us probably would not have wanted to be in that particular place or to have seen what Ezekiel saw that day. But he knew that it was from God. He was conscious of the fact that *"the hand of the Lord was upon [him],"* that it *"carried [him] out in the Spirit of the Lord,"* and that it *"set [him] down in the midst of the valley which was full of bones."* He may not have understood it all yet, but he trusted God and knew that there was a divine purpose for what was happening to him.

Ezekiel Took A Closer Look

Next, the Spirit *"caused [Ezekiel] to pass by them round about."* In other words Ezekiel now took a little tour around so that he could get a good view of all of the bones in this great valley. His observations were that they were *"very many"* and that they were *"very dry."*

To dispel any doubt about what kind of bones these were, the Amplified Bible renders this second verse in this way:

Understanding the Seed

And He caused me to pass round about among them, and behold, there were very many [human bones] in the open valley or plain, and behold, they were very dry. (AMP)

These were not the bones of wild animal, buzzards, or even domestic animals. They were human bones. Once this truth had dawned on Ezekiel, then the Lord asked him that question: *"Son of man, can these bones live?"*

What a question! Ezekiel didn't know the answer. All he knew to say was, *"O Lord God, You know."*

It's a Valid Question Still Today

Still today people are asking, "Can that person ever be raised up again, that person who once walked and talked with the Lord and had a great and powerful ministry ... until something came along that seemed bigger and better to them, and they yielded to it and fell?" Some of the most famous of them have received a lot of free advertisement because their failure was broadcast all over the world. Millions of households suddenly knew about it.

Many have wondered: "How could that happen to a real man or woman of God?" If you are one of those who think like that, let me set you straight. You don't know when something may come your way that will prove to be the biggest fight of your life, the greatest temptation to you, and you will need to call on God for His help with it.

If we are wise, we will avoid talking about the failures of others, because we don't know what fights might be coming our way. One day we might have to eat the words we now throw around so freely. There are many hurting people in the Body of Christ, and they need our prayers, not our criticisms. Many have fallen. They are down, and they cannot seem to get back up. Some walked away because they were hurt. They were not lesser people. They were just like you and me, ministers of the Living God.

Pastors, Teachers, and Evangelists

Some of those who have fallen were pastors, some of them were teachers, and some of them were evangelists. Some were just housewives or mothers, but they were all carrying out the beautiful plan of the Lord for their lives when something came their way that they were unable to overcome in that moment.

But, just because these people were unable to overcome in that particular moment doesn't mean that they're not overcomers. It doesn't mean that they cannot get up and go on. It doesn't mean that God will no longer touch them. Can God bring life to them again? Oh, yes, He can!

Start Prophesying It into Being

The sight Ezekiel saw was so overwhelming that he wasn't sure what the answer was, so he answered: "I don't know, Lord. Only You know whether life can come again to these bones." But what did God answer to that? He told Ezekiel to start prophesying it into being.

There is no fallen person that God cannot raise up (perhaps with the exception of one who has blasphemed the

Holy Spirit). But blasphemy of the Holy Spirit is the only unpardonable sin.

Divorce Is Not the Unpardonable Sin

Divorce is not an unpardonable sin, and it's time we stop acting like it is. It is always better for a minister to remain faithful to his or her original spouse, but God knows how to reach down and put His Spirit and life in one who has divorced and/or remarried. If He chooses to raise them up again and give them new hope, who are we to continue to condemn them?

The Scriptures declare:

For the gifts and calling of God are without repentance.
Romans 11:29

You and I claim this passage over our own lives, so why should others not claim it too? Should we amend the verse to say: **The gifts and calling of God are without repentance, except in the case of _____**? Only God has that right, and He hasn't done it. Divorce is not the end of your life, and divorce is not the end of your calling either.

For far too many years, when a minister failed in a certain way, we considered their ministry to be over and all doors closed to them. But nothing is over until God says it's over.

Our God is merciful. He is full of grace. He is able to take hold of a fallen one and lift them up again. He is able to take a discouraged one and give them reason to stand again. He is able to take a broken one and put them back together again. And when He does it, they will be better than they were before.

"Can these bones live again?"

"Oh, Lord, you know."

Yes, He knows. He knows that nothing is impossible with Him.

"You're Ugly"

There is a joke I love to tell about a store owner in New York who had a talking bird. He would place the bird out in front of his store, and the bird, which had an amazing vocabulary, would make comments to the people who passed by. He told the women on their way to and from their offices how beautiful they were. That is ... most of them. Whenever he saw one particular woman coming, he would look her up and down and then say, "You're ugly."

As you can imagine, this bothered the woman, especially since she overheard the bird telling other women how beautiful they were. Invariably his comment to her was always the same, "You're ugly." This went on until she was so offended that she decided to confront the owner about it, and she did, relaying to him exactly what the bird had been doing.

The owner was embarrassed by what the bird had done, and he promised to do his best to correct his behavior. Later that day, he spoke with the bird and threatened him if he continued to insult the woman.

The next morning, as usual, that woman came walking by the shop. There were others in front of her, and she overheard the bird saying to each of them in turn, "You're so beautiful. You're so beautiful."

When the woman came face to face with the bird, she couldn't wait to hear what he would say. When he saw her, he lowered his head for a moment, then he looked up at her and said, "You know! You know!"

I think sometimes this is what the Holy Spirit is saying to us. We somehow think that we're so beautiful and we've done such wonderful things for the Lord, and all the while He is trying to convict us of something in our character or actions that is not so nice and needs attention. You know! You know!

We no longer want to hear the truth because it hurts too much, so He just looks down at us and says, "You know!" It's time to get those things right. It's time to repent and get our lives straightened out. Then we'll be beautiful, and we'll hear the Spirit of the Lord saying, "You're beautiful now. You're beautiful!" And we'll rejoice that we have done the right thing.

Now, It's Your Turn

So what was God's answer to Ezekiel's doubt about whether or not the bones could live again? He was to start prophesying it into existence. And, today, God is calling you by name and inviting you to prophesy His will into existence in the lives of those around you. Prophesy, and change your world!

The Scriptures teach:

The testimony of Jesus is the spirit of prophecy.
                                        Revelation 19:10

You have the testimony of Jesus in you, so you also have the spirit of prophecy.
Paul wrote to the Corinthian church:

For ye may all prophesy one by one, that all may learn, and all may be comforted.   1 Corinthians 14:31

He didn't say that all of us are prophets, but he did say that we can all prophesy. No one is excluded, so that includes you.

Ezekiel Obeyed

Ezekiel was to prophesy to those dry bones. Some of us would not even like to see them, let alone prophesy to them. But Ezekiel obeyed:

So I prophesied as I was commanded.   Ezekiel 37:7

You can't bring dead bones to life, but you can prophesy. Do what God has called you to do, and He will do the rest (what you can't do).

What Should He Say?

What should a prophet say to dry bones? Fortunately the Lord told Ezekiel exactly what to say:

Prophesy upon these bones, and say unto them, O ye dry bones, hear the word of the Lord. *Thus saith the* Lord *God unto these bones; Behold, I will cause breath to enter into you, and ye shall live: and I will lay sinews upon you, and will bring up flesh upon you, and cover you with skin, and put breath in you, and ye shall live; and ye shall know that I am the* Lord. Ezekiel 37:4-6

Ezekiel's obedience was not only in the fact that he was willing to prophesy to dry bones, but also in the fact that God had told him exactly what to say. He did it, and he said it, and it produced a shaking and a coming together.

The Coming Together

Now, I want us to think about this for a moment. There were many bones, and those bones were very dry. They had no more meat on them, and they were bleached white from the sun. That was about as extreme as you can get, and yet the moment Ezekiel prophesied the word of the Lord something began to happen. Those dry bones heard his prophecy.

If dry bones can hear the Word of the Lord and respond, what is happening with you and me? Should our ears, that are still living, not be even more attuned to God, so that we can hear His voice and respond?

Ignore What People Think or Say

Ezekiel was every bit as much human as we are, and he must have been thinking to himself, "My Lord, if people see me out here talking to these dry bones and telling them they're going to live, what will they think of me?" If we're going to do God's work, we need to get over what people think or say. If you speak words to dead things, and especially if you speak words to dead things that others want to keep dead, you will not be well understood or appreciated. Get used to it. Ignore the naysayers.

Begin by Resurrecting Your Prayer Life

One of the dead things in our lives that needs to be resurrected is our prayer life. The enemy attacks it every way he can. He tries to make you think of all the negatives:

- There's no excitement in it.
- There's no joy in it.
- It has become a chore that actually seems to hinder you as you press forward into new places in God.

I want to encourage you in this regard. It may seem that you are making no headway in prayer. It may feel like you have a ton of bricks on top of you or like something or someone heavy is sitting on your chest. But if you will keep on keeping on, keep on pressing in, keep on talking to the Lord, keep on speaking those words that He gives you over that situation, there shall be a performance of His Word that shall come to pass in your life. I guarantee it. Dead things will begin to come to life.

Understanding the Seed
Beyond Mere Life

Ezekiel's prophecy went far beyond mere life: God said through him: *"And I will lay sinews upon you, and will bring up flesh upon you, and cover you with skin, and put breath in you, and ye shall live; and ye shall know that I am the Lord."* Wow! And he was talking to bare, parched bones.

We cannot emphasize too much the importance of getting close to God, hearing His voice, and thus finding out what His plan is for the person we are ministering to. Only then can we open our mouths and declare to them what will be. We are not to add anything to it or take anything away from it. God's words bring life, so we must speak them word-for-word as He gives them to us.

Prophecy is God putting His words in our mouths and us speaking them. If we are faithful to speak His words, saying exactly what He has said to us, there will always be results. If, on the other hand, we happen to know something about the person we are prophesying to, for instance something that happened many years ago, and we allow our personal knowledge to influence what we say, we can err.

God wants to raise that person up, and all you can think about is what you heard about them years ago. In some cases, you may have firsthand knowledge of what happened to this person. You were there. You know that they fell. Now, however, God wants to raise them up, and He wants to use you to do it., He will use your voice and your hands. Therefore, as ministers of Christ, we must be able to lay aside our personal knowledge, so that God's will can be spoken and performed. This requires asking Him to make our hearts and minds like a blackboard that has been erased. Then, when we speak, we will speak only what He says, not adding anything to it. When this is true, just wait and see what God will do. You will be amazed, as I'm sure Ezekiel was that day.

Refuse to Listen to Gossip

When God has shown you that He desires to raise others up, refuse to listen to fresh gossip about them. The enemy will send those who have the "buts." "But ... did you know? But ... did you hear?" When God has spoken, let all "buts" be buried. Let nothing hinder God from doing His work.

No Hope?

If the person you are called to prophesy to cannot be raised up, then neither can you. If there's no hope for them, then there's no hope for you either.

Our God is alive, and He is the God of resurrection. You and I, as ministers of the Lord Jesus Christ, must allow people who are down to get up. Give God a chance to change them.

Some say, "Well, they're going to have to prove it to me first." How can you prove something if you're never given a chance to do it?

People make mistakes, and so do you. You have made some, and you're still making some. Let others find their way back, just as the Lord allows you to find your way back. Allow them to get up. Give them room. Give them opportunity. Give them time to tell what God is doing in their lives. You would want others to do it for you, so you must do it for others.

Ezekiel prophesied as he was commanded, and you can do the same thing, regardless of the circumstances.

That Was Enough

Once Ezekiel had prophesied, there was not much else he could do, but that was enough. Now God began to do His part:

So I prophesied as I was commanded: and as I prophesied, there was a noise, and behold a shaking, and the bones came together, bone to his bone. And when I beheld, lo, the sinews and the flesh came up upon them, and the skin covered them above: but there was no breath in them.

Ezekiel 37:7-8

Can you imagine the sight? How wonderful! Ezekiel's vision was coming to pass. He could hear it. Bones were moving and shaking, and then the bones began to come together, bone to his bone.

What a miracle! A bone from one person was not joined to a bone from another person. Each bone found its own matching skeleton and was joined to it. God had created man in the beginning, but these men were being recreated right there before the prophet's eyes, beginning with their skeleton.

Next, the prophet watched as sinews and flesh came upon those bones, and then as skin covered it all. Wow! I don't know how long this all took, but in any amount of time, this was an incredible creative miracle. Still, the verse ends on a negative note. After all of this, there was still *"no breath in them."*

No Breath in Them

This was like going back to Genesis and hearing God say, "Let us make man," and then seeing Him take the dust of the earth and shape a man from it. (We didn't even come from dirt; we came from dust.)

Now God had a beautiful structure in the image He desired, but again, there was no breath in it. So then God put His own mouth upon that clay-like substance and breathed into it, and man suddenly became flesh and bone, a living soul. His name was Adam, and we're all descended from him. Praise God for the miracle of creation.

We're now the bones God is concerned about, the Body of Christ, the household of Israel, and He is breathing afresh upon our lives to lift us up and make of us what only He can envision.

But, again, these bones, now come together and covered with flesh, had no breath in them. Sometimes something happens to us, as God's people, and we get the breath knocked out of us. But God is still the great Creator, and He is willing and able to breathe on us again and bring to us a fresh touch of His life.

Understanding the Seed
Not Yet Complete

Ezekiel prophesied, and he saw what he had prophesied come to pass. But it was not yet complete. Now God told him to prophesy again:

> *Then said he unto me, Prophesy unto the wind, prophesy, son of man, and say to the wind, Thus saith the Lord God; Come from the four winds, O breath, and breathe upon these slain, that they may live.*   Ezekiel 37:9

Oh, great! First he's prophesying to dead bones, and now he's prophesying to the wind! But the Amplified Bible says it this way:

> *Then said He to me, Prophesy to the breath and the spirit, son of man, and say to the breath and the spirit, Thus says the Lord God: Come from the four winds, O breath and spirit, and breathe upon these slain that they may live.* (AMP)

So maybe Ezekiel wasn't prophesying to the wind as we understand it. Whatever the case, he obeyed. That's the important thing. And when you and I are obedient to God to speak His words, there will be a performance of that word in our lives, as there was with Ezekiel:

> *So I prophesied as he commanded me, and the breath came into them, and they lived, and stood up upon their feet, an exceeding great army.*   Ezekiel 37:10

This Is the Hour

I believe that this is the hour for the slain of the Lord to come forth, an exceeding great army. They may not be in the grave already, but they might as well be. They are dead — dead to the Church, dead to the Spirit of God, dead to the Kingdom. They have been embarrassed and condemned so long and so hard that they have no more spirit in them to rise up. Nothing in them desires to read the Word of God, and they have even lost all hope that God will hear them if they pray.

You know some of these people. They live around you in your community. Some you may have only heard about and not known them personally. Whatever the case, why not pick up the phone and call them and tell them that there is hope in God? Tell them that He can lift them up once again, that He desires to breathe on them again and that their best days are yet to come.

They may feel like they're ready for the hangman, but God says their best days are ahead. He is going to raise them up, restore them, and bring them back to the place of magnifying and glorifying His wonderful and powerful name. The call that was upon their lives will never be rescinded. It is as fresh today as it ever has been. Let God breathe upon His people who are slain.

Let Him Breathe on You

As a family, we cry out to God to bring us revival. In the same way, let us now expect the breath of God to come into our midst, breathe upon us, and take away the deadness that exists on the inside of us as individuals. Let it no longer be going to church just because church is going on. Let it no longer be speaking a message just because it is expected of us. Let it no longer be forcing ourselves to do the right thing just because we're Christians and that's what Christians do. May our tithing no longer be a ritual without feeling or purpose. Present every dead thing to God for resurrection. He wants to breathe new life into them.

One Pastor's Testimony

One pastor testified that everything was going well in his church for a time. The congregation was growing, and God was working among them, and it was a joy to minister. Then the problems began, and they were not small problems. After a while, it got so bad that he dreaded having to preach. He dreaded having to teach a class. The problems and worrying about how to resolve the problems began to affect his relationship with his wife so severely that they were considering divorce. In desperation he decided to go to one of the places experiencing revival.

At first, he thought he was going just to observe, just to see what was happening, and so he sat way up at the top, far from the platform or the altar activities. Eventually, however, he felt convicted and went forward and got prayed for. When he returned to his room that night, he didn't notice any big change. But the next day he noticed that he had a desire to lift his hands to the Lord a little. Something was happening.

It Changed His Marriage and His Church

He had promised his wife that he would be home that day for their regular church service, so he called her to say that he was on his way and told her a little about what he had experienced. When he arrived at the church, the service was already in progress, and his wife was on the platform. When she saw him, she got up and started toward him, and he started toward her. They met halfway and fell into each others' arms, and when they did that, the power of God hit the place, and revival started. Everybody was excited because the pastors were excited.

Church that day was anything but the "usual." It kept going into the late afternoon, then into the night, and on into the next night. The testimonies that came out of that church were that people who had been saved for many years, faithful people, men and women in leadership, saw a difference when God came and breathed upon them. It's different when God comes and opens your heart to Him.

Now, you're no longer attending services because you have to go. You're no longer giving tithes just because you know it's the right thing to do. You're not sitting there with your arms folded waiting for church to be over so that you can go get something to eat. God has placed an excitement on the inside of you, and now you want to go. In fact, you can't wait for church to get started.

The pastor testified that before this they had always been careful to close their services early out of respect for those who had to get up and go to work the next day. Now their services were lasting until after midnight, and this was going on night after night.

The people wanted to be there, and they wanted to be careful to do what God wanted in each service because His breath was moving upon them. When He pours out His Spirit upon us and His power is evident among us, we are compelled to lay aside our formalities and stop doing things as we have grown accustomed to doing them and accept God's ways.

WE FACE THE SAME DANGER

We always face that same danger on the campground. If we just have forty-five minutes of praise and worship as usual, forty-five minutes of preaching or teaching as usual, and another forty-five minutes of praying for the people as usual, and then we all head to the snack bar to eat before going home to bed, what are we accomplishing? God wants to reverse our traditions so that a snack bar is no longer calling us.

Having to get up the next morning must no longer dominate our thinking. We need God to put such an excitement in our souls that we will not only be personally consumed with what He is doing; we will also invite others and watch to see what God does for them.

Let's tell them, "Come and see what God is doing. Come and be a part of something very exciting. Come and be changed." If we get changed first, then others will surely be changed too.

It Worked for Ezekiel

When Ezekiel prophesied as he was commanded, then God did what He had promised to do. Today we need God to move in our midst in a supernatural way, and when He does, the dead will suddenly arise and stand tall among us.

In Ezekiel's day, *"They lived."* They had been dead, very dead, but now they were alive, and together they formed *"an exceeding great army."*

The Meaning of It

Now God showed Ezekiel the meaning of all that he had just seen:

Then he said unto me, Son of man, these bones are the whole house of Israel: behold, they say, Our bones are dried, and our hope is lost: we are cut off for our parts. Therefore prophesy and say unto them, Thus saith the Lord God; Behold, O my people, I will open your graves, and cause you to come up out of your graves, and bring you into the land of Israel. And ye shall know that I am the Lord, when I have opened your graves, O my people, and brought you up out of your graves, and shall put my spirit in you, and ye shall live, and I shall place you in your own land: then shall ye know that I the Lord have spoken it, and performed it, saith the Lord.

Ezekiel 37:11-14

The bones had been symbolic of God's people, *"the whole house of Israel."* If Ezekiel prophesied God's words to His people and they responded, what had happened to the dry bones of Ezekiel's vision would also happen to them. They were feeling dry, feeling that their hope was lost, and that they were cut off from their other parts. Only God's words could restore them.

What To Do?

So what do we do when we encounter dead things and dead people? We usually shrink back, horrified at their terrible condition, and wondering if they can ever change. What we need to do is begin to prophesy life to them, and see what God will do.

In our time, an army of God's servants has been sent forth to call the scattered and damaged people of Israel back home, and they have responded. God has done for them all that He promised to do. Our concern today is not for the physical House of Israel, but for the slain among the Body of Christ worldwide.

Far too many members of His Body are down, disappointed, disgraced, and discouraged. Things have not been going well for them. But the same God who has raised up the House of Israel and called her scattered members from the four corners of the earth to return to the land and be blessed, is even now sending forth a call to the fallen members of the Body of Christ to come home.

Could He possibly do less for the believers in Christ than He has done for His people Israel? These are those who have been called by His name and are washed in the precious blood of Jesus, and He loves them no less. He has called us the light of the world and has predestined us to be His voice in the earth in these last days. He has called us to be the ones to go for Him, representing Him in the fullness of who He is. He has called us to speak, teach, declare, and prophesy His Word. In His name, we must now take the hand of the one who is down, lift them up and tell them, "God will restore you. God will bring you back to the fullness of that for which He has called you. You are important to the Body of Christ, and it doesn't matter what you have done in the past. God is bigger than all your failure."

Is This Right?

Is this the right thing to do? Absolutely. When Jesus hung on the cross more than two thousand years ago, He took all of our sin upon Himself. Today, He is still taking our sins — if we let Him — and He washes away all the stains in our lives and makes us new.

So why not be an instrument to help someone else? Encourage them by saying, "God is going to help you. He's not finished with you yet. He's got something for you to do, and this is your day to get up and go forward."

They may not go very far at first. They may not even feel like taking that first step. But if something has begun to stir on the inside of them, it won't be long before they'll lift up their hands and their heads, they'll get back into the church, into the Bible, and into that place of magnifying and glorifying the name of the Lord. We are His people, so let us do His work in the days ahead.

The "Greater Works"

God is calling us all to be strengthened, to pray for each other, and to declare afresh that we shall do *"greater works than these"* because Jesus has gone to the Father (John 14:12). I am convinced that one of those *"greater works"* is reaching out to those who once walked in light but now seem to have no hope and be instrumental in bringing them back to that place of blessing.

Some of them are on drugs. Some are into alcohol. Some of them have even turned to prostitution. Their life is even more horrible because they remember what it was like to walk with the Lord and be counted among His people.

But Jesus taught us to be merciful as He is merciful, to be kind as He is kind, to be forgiving as He is forgiving. We are to receive others as He has received us.

Receive Them As He Received Us

Aren't you glad that He received you? Aren't you glad that He did not stop receiving you even when you failed Him? Aren't you glad that He drew you to Himself, and when you couldn't get up on your own, He reached down, picked you up, and helped you to get on your feet again? Because of this, can you and I not now become His representatives to the fallen?

Don't just preach at them. Don't shake the Bible in their faces. Tell them, "Jesus loves you and knows where you are, and still He says to you, 'I'm going to raise you up, and this is your day.' " If you will reach out to them in that loving and kind way, the river of God that is on the inside of you will flow out and bring life and hope to their souls.

Isaiah declared:

The L ORD God hath given me the tongue of the learned, that I should know how to speak a word in season to him that is weary. Isaiah 50:4

If you will use that tongue to bless others, it will bring them out. It will strengthen them. It will give them hope.

If you're not convinced, stick your tongue out to the Lord today and say, "Lord, heal my tongue. Let it be filled with mercy and kindness. Let it be filled with peaceful words. Let me be one who will help somebody else to get up and run the course that You have called them to. Amen!"

WILL YOU GO?

When God speaks to us and asks us, "Will you go for Me?" He is not asking us to go to some other country on a sight-seeing tour. He is not asking us to go to another city just to see what it looks like or to take in its historic locations. He is saying to us, "Will you go for Me? Will you go preach and teach My Word? Will you go and reach out your hand and touch someone with My love, My life, and

My power? Will you go and be gentle and kind and help someone who is down, someone who is wounded and broken? Will you be bread that is broken for Me? Will you be like wine that is poured out for Me?"

The psalmist David cried out unto the Lord:

Thy gentleness hath made me great.   Psalm 18:35

David was already king, but he didn't see his position as king or his acts of valor in battle as his source of greatness. No, he was great because the gentle God lived in him.

God had been gentle with David on many occasions, and He expected David to be gentle with others. David knew that he had not always lived up to his calling and had not always deserved God's gentleness, and yet God had always been gentle with him. No doubt that is what led David to take pity on Saul when he could have killed him and felt justified in doing so. Instead, he let him go, thus honoring the anointing of the then ruler.

Let Them Go

There are some wrongs that you and I need to let go of and leave at the altar. People have said things about you, hurt you, disappointed you, even lied about you. What should you do? Let it go. It doesn't matter. It's not worth being upset about. And if you don't let it go, it will eat you up and destroy you. Forgive that person. Set them free. In so doing, you will set yourself free.

Yes, this is all for ministers. Yes, we are the ministers of God, His representatives in the earth. But that means that we are to carry on His work. While He was here, what did He do? He not only cast out devils. He not only healed the sick, opened the blind eyes, and made the lame to walk. He also said to the woman caught in adultery:

Neither do I condemn thee: go, and sin no more.
John 8:11

Let this be our attitude as well, as we go forth to raise up the dead bones of our age.

Amen!

Chapter 2

Becoming Servant of All
by Dr. Harold McDougal

Calvary Campground has been a great blessing to me through the years. I first went there and met the founders way back in 1964. I had met Ruth Ward Heflin, their daughter, in India earlier that year, where she and I ministered together in several wonderful conventions and crusades.

After I came back to the United States, I wanted to meet the entire Heflin family, so I went to Ashland that December. From that time on, we were all very close friends: Wallace, Sr. and Edith Heflin, the Founders of the camp ministry, and Wallace Jr. and Ruth, their children.

All of the Heflins visited me in the various mission fields I served in and helped us bring revival to those places. Mother Heflin visited me only once, as she often stayed home holding down the fort while the others traveled in ministry. She was also occupied raising the Henderson grandchildren, children of Betty Heflin Henderson, the oldest Heflin child, who, unfortunately, I never knew. She had died that summer. Ruth was a part of my wedding and Wallace Jr. always told people that I was the brother he never had.

They are all gone now. When Wallace Sr. died, the family asked me to conduct his funeral. When Wallace Jr. died, I was again asked to conduct his funeral. Before Ruth died, she gave me detailed instructions for her funeral, and we carried those out. At the same time she told me what to do for her funeral, she told me that Jane Lowder, originally a farm girl from Stanly County, North Carolina, was the person they trusted to carry on this ministry, and she has done a wonderful job with it.

CPT in the Philippines

When I went out to a more permanent missionary work, beginning in the Philippines, we soon established a camp where people could come and be blessed and not have to pay for the privilege. And then we challenged them to go back and be a blessing to others, and the results were wonderful. Our camp was named after Calvary Campground because that camp inspired us to do it and showed us that it was possible. The Heflin family and their camp ministry always challenged us to greater things in God, and I'm so grateful for having known them.

I was blessed to travel many times with Brother Heflin Jr. and to participate with him in crusades in many countries. It was because of his vision that we were led to South America and Ecuador in particular, where we spent seven wonderfully fruitful years. Then, when I was led to go to Sierra Leone to help establish a Bible training center there in Freetown, he took a large group and conducted a crusade. It was a great kick-off for the Bible school that followed.

My First Campmeeting

I attended my first campmeeting at CPT in the summer of 1965, and I loved it so much that I stayed on for many weeks afterward helping to build some of the early camp housing. It was early that next year when the Lord took us to the Philippines. We had met our Filipino contact at the camp that summer.

I was blessed to be one of the campmeeting speakers first in 1969. Then, when I was living in Ecuador, I came up nearly every summer for conferences in the States, and so I was at camp more often. After I returned to this country, I drove the three hours from our home in Maryland most every weekend that camp was in session, and also for the special conferences. When I began volunteering to upgrade the camp computer systems, software, and bookkeeping systems, I was there even more.

For one year, I lived in Ashland and worked full time with the camp. We were teaching Bible school classes, along with the other camp activities. That was before I got so busy with publishing. Then, two years before Brother Heflin died, the Lord spoke to me to give him two days a week to help organize his personal papers, and generally serve as the administrator for the many ministries he carried on. I didn't have any idea then that he would leave us so early, but I have always been very thankful that I obeyed God and gave those two years.

A Special Atmosphere

It was a blessing to again be in the camp for the ministers' meetings where these messages first came forth. To me, this type of meeting is one of the most wonderful and important we can have. It's important to have crusades that bring in the lost. It's important to have regular church meetings, where people are rooted and grounded in the Word. It's wonderful to come to campmeetings like the ones conducted at CPT, where we can be challenged and motivated. Personally, I've never gone there that I wasn't challenged to do more for God and lifted to a new level in Him.

It's wonderful to have any type of meeting where Christ is exalted, but there is something special about a meeting of ministers. We are those who have a special and unique calling upon our lives to serve Him, to be His voice in the earth, to carry out His eternal plans. When we get together, therefore, there is a special anointing present. There is a special presence of the Lord. And in meetings such as this, we can say things that we cannot say at most any other time because no one would understand what we were talking about. The reason is that spiritual children cannot be expected to comprehend the adult conversations we can have among the more mature ministers, servants of the Lord. Our lives were changed in those meetings, and we were happy to have been a part of such a historic event.

Praise Where Praise Is Due

As you can see, I love Calvary Campground, I loved the people who gave their lives to make it a place where people could be changed, and I also honor those who continue to give their lives there. Theirs is not an easy life, but they will be richly rewarded.

Thank God for such a place as this. Anyone can go there and not have to worry about paying for every single thing. The camp provides a comfortable place to sleep, and they feed everyone — physically and spiritually. What more could we ask for? Thank God for those who keep the place running, keeping the electric bill paid and the heat (or air-conditioning) on. Thank God for those who are willing to perform the many arduous physical tasks that are necessary so that the hungry can be blessed.

"A Certain Disciple"

My message for this chapter is from my favorite book of the Bible, Acts of the Apostles. It begins in this way:

Now there was a certain disciple at Damascus named Ananias; and to him the Lord said in a vision, "Ananias." Acts 9:10, NKJV

When any of us conducts an evangelistic service, it is a wonderful thing. Lost are found, and we rejoice with the angels of Heaven. But when you can minister to someone who has a call to ministry themselves, we just might be raising up the next Paul of Tarsus.

Paul, or Saul, as he was then known, was a man who would change the world, a man who would write over half of the New Testament, a man who would establish many of the first Gentile churches, and God was calling Ananias to minister to him. You cannot know what the person you are ministering to may someday do, but God does.

Every soul is important, but it is so much more powerful to minister to one who has the potential of reaching thousands of others for God. That's the reason working with ministers has always been my favorite ministry.

BEGINNING IN EVANGELISM

We all start out in evangelism in one form or another, and it was no different with me. I loved evangelism, loved going to places no one else was going and reaching people no one else was reaching. Evangelism and miracles go together, and it was always so exciting watching God work His miracles and seeing those miracles open the minds and hearts of many to receive Him. There's nothing quite like it.

During my years overseas as a missionary, I particularly loved going into the high mountain places, where entire villages accepted Christ. It was hard getting there, but it was well worth it all. The mountains were beautiful, and the people of those mountain villages were beautiful too. Having been born in the mountains of West Virginia, I had a special love for that ministry.

I also loved going to the remote islands, where few missionaries dared to venture. I was particularly blessed to go to the island of Hibusong in the Philippines. It took five days of boat travel to get there, and we had to transfer from one boat to a smaller boat, to an even smaller boat, and so on. But once there, it was a treat. What a beautiful island! And what beautiful people!

A Tiny Island in the Pacific

The island was small. I could walk around it in two hours, and when I climbed to the top of the hill, I could view the entire island from that one spot. It was a breathtaking view. There were no roads and no electricity on the entire island. It was a tropical paradise.

The population of Hibusong was not large at the time, a few hundred people, and yet God raised up twenty young people from that place who went all over the world preaching His Word, and many of them continue to do so today. Evangelism is wonderful.

I Was Not As Comfortable As a Pastor

Because of my temperament, I was not nearly as comfortable being a pastor, but I had no choice in the matter. After we began to establish churches in unreached areas through our evangelistic crusades, we had no place to send the people who were being saved. We could not just abandon them. What could we do?

It was a lot like having children. It's a very exciting process, but then after they are born, we have to accept the fact that we are responsible to care for them for many years to come. We can't expect someone else to care for our children, when we are their rightful parents. We can't visit a neighbor and say, "I have been blessed with this precious child, and I want to give him to you to raise." No, we're the parents, so we have to parent the children God gives us, whether we seem to have parental potential or not. In the same way, pastoral work was forced upon us, whether we liked it or felt particularly qualified for it or not.

As our evangelistic team was raising up churches in new places, it suddenly dawned on us that these people needed further instruction. They needed regular care. They had to be fed. And there was no one else to do it. Suddenly we were all going different directions on service days to care for these emerging congregations. Ready or not, we had to become pastors, simply because there was no one else to do it.

We Had a Lot to Learn

Pastors face every type of challenge, because they deal with every type of person imaginable. This means you have to be ready for whatever comes. It was a great challenge, and it meant that we had a lot to learn, and we had to learn it quickly. It wasn't enough now to preach how to come to the feet of Jesus. Our message had to go far beyond that. Pastors have to teach many others many things, and none of us can teach something we haven't first learned ourselves. If we don't know what we believe and why, how can we teach our children? A teacher is first a learner.

This was what Jesus meant when He said:

Go ye therefore, and teach all nations, baptizing them in the name of the Father, and of the Son, and of the Holy Ghost: teaching them to observe all things whatsoever I have commanded you: and, lo, I am with you always, even unto the end of the world.   Matthew 28:19-20

"Teaching them to observe" what? "All things whatsoever I have commanded you." And who was to teach all those things? Those who are called to go to all nations and preach the Gospel. The preaching of the Gospel may only take moments, but the teaching of all the things we have been commanded surely will take much more of our time. That's why we like the first part of this Great Commission and do not like the second part nearly as much. But they are part of the same Great Commission.

Teaching Is a Privilege

Teaching those whom the Lord places under us, our spiritual children, is more than a privilege; it is our duty. And we must teach them everything the Lord has taught us. That takes more than fifteen minutes. It takes more than one sitting. It takes more than a week, a month, or even a year. It requires the investment of a lot of time and effort on our part, and a lot of patience, perseverance, and prayer.

Our reward is a mature person who can do the works of God. Until then you will be required to change a lot of diapers, wipe a lot of messy noses, burp a lot of babies, and feed people who sometimes don't really want to be fed. They want ice cream and cake and don't understand why they have to eat what's on the table. You have to patiently teach them and help them along, and it's a big (and sometimes thankless) job.

I Found My Passion

Although I didn't feel comfortable in the role of pastor, I counted it a privilege and did it with joy ... until He raised up others to do it. I was grateful when that time came because, in the meantime, I had found my first love. I still occasionally did crusades, and I filled the post of pastor when needed, but I had found what I love to do best and feel most comfortable doing, and that was raising up the next generation of ministers to carry on the work, the modern-day Sauls, Phillips and Peters.

I started organizing and teaching Bible schools out of necessity. We needed more workers, and every other servant of God had the same problem. I found that I loved it. It became my passion, and I did it on several continents.

In the process, I was led to seek out the very best candidates and then spend weeks and months with them in prayer and fasting, and in serious study of the Word of God and its practical application. I loved it. I could stand for hours before them pouring into their lives and never feel tired. Many of my books were developed through teaching others in this way.

The Rewards of Teaching

I was rewarded when many whom I had trained went on to win more souls than I had ever won, establish more churches than I had ever been able to establish, and do greater miracles than I had ever been blessed to do. Many of them are over great ministries today in many nations.

When I was just twenty-one, I was privileged to stand before ten thousand people in South India and minister. My spiritual sons and daughters have preached before much larger crowds. They have done greater exploits.

A Great Example

One of my spiritual sons from Sierra Leone, Desmond Thomas, studied under me in the Bible school in Freetown in the early 1980s. As noted earlier, I went there with Brother Wallace Heflin and a great team from the Ashland camp. After the crusade and the meetings in the churches, everyone else left for home, but I stayed on for six weeks. It was Christmas time, and I was away from my family, but the people of Sierra Leone became my family.

During those weeks, I worked with the men and women who would teach after I had gone, and I carefully screened and selected the students. We didn't want just anyone. We wanted serious people who would seek God and learn quickly so that they could become effective servants for God.

We only had about twenty graduates from that first program, but thankfully most of those are still in the ministry today. Desmond was one of them. He went on to establish two churches there in his native Sierra Leone. Then war broke out, and the Lord sent him to London. In London, he established a great church among the African exiles.

Eventually things quieted down in Sierra Leone, and he felt led to go back. This time, the Lord told him to establish a Bible training center to raise up more leaders for the work in his native land. After he had started the school, he visited us in Baton Rouge, Louisiana, and told us what was happening in his life. He also invited us to come and see the work in Sierra Leone. Time passed and he communicated with us that he would soon be ready to have his first graduation. Could we come and be part of it? We were only too happy to go.

What a thrill it was to see more than sixty Sierra Leonean students achieving their dream of having prepared themselves for the ministry. I had helped to train twenty, and one of those was Desmond. Now he had trained more than sixty. That's what God does.

THE PRINCIPLE OF MULTIPLICATION

It is because of this principle of multiplication that the ministry of raising up others has been so dear to my heart. I have loved putting these same teachings into books and having them translated into many languages and seeing them dispersed among the nations. To God be all the glory.

In recent years, my time has been more dedicated to this publishing ministry, but I love it because every day I get to work with anointed teachers and preachers, getting their materials into print to bless others. They have such exciting testimonies and powerful teachings that can and do change lives. I am blessed to be part of it. Someone you touch just might become the next Billy Graham, the next Saul of Tarsus.

Looking Closer

Let's look at this passage in Acts a little closer. There are some important lessons here for all of us.

First, we note that the Lord spoke to Ananias in a vision, and then he had something to do. This is important. God has many ways of speaking today, so He may speak to you differently, but we must be careful not to make a move without first hearing from Him. Why is that? Because this ministry is God's, not ours. Those people you are working with are priceless souls that He has redeemed from perdition. Handle them with care. The church you are involved with is part of His Church, and He is the Head over that Church, not you. When you are in ministry, you cannot do whatever you would like to do. He is over all and above all.

You, therefore, cannot decide what you will do and how you will do it. It doesn't work that way. You may do it, but it will not be anointed, it will not be blessed, and it will not be fruitful. You will not have the same impact as you might have had if you had waited until you heard the voice of God.

Whether you hear from God in a vision, a dream, a prophecy, audibly, or some other way, that is not important. What is important is that you do nothing without first knowing what He wants done. Get God's mind before attempting anything in ministry.

The Tendency to Copy Others

What often happens is that we see someone else doing something for God, and it looks good to us, so we imitate them (or we try to). I was guilty of this as a young preacher, still in high school. I heard preachers that I loved, and I tried to do things the same way they did. I tried to use some of the same Bible verses, the same phrases, and the same hand gestures they used, but it just didn't work for me. Then I got on my face before God and received His touch for my life, and that worked.

I was blessed to be raised in the country, and there were forests nearby, so when I got serious with God, I would go to the forest and lie on my face in the leaves and call on Him. There could not have been a better place to do it. He was there, and He began to speak to me and show me what He wanted for my life. I didn't need to imitate someone else.

If you are not hearing from God, I can promise you that it's not His fault. He is faithful to speak to those who listen for Him. If you're not hearing from God, get a little closer, lean on His breast, feel His heartbeat. Do a little more fasting. Pray with more seriousness. Do whatever it takes to hear the voice of God because He does speak, and His words to you will make all the difference in your life and ministry.

Ananias Answered

God called to Ananias, and Ananias answered:

And he said, "Here I am, Lord."   Acts 9:10

This man was not too busy or too preoccupied with other things. His thoughts were not consumed with how he was going to pay his bills or how he was going to resolve difficult family situations. In fact, we know nothing about the man's family and that's because it was not important for us to know. Whatever his family situation, Ananias had time to talk to God, and he had time to listen as God talked to him.

"Here I Am, Lord"

I love what Ananias answered God that day: *"Here I am, Lord."* It reminds me of the Spanish phrase *"a la orden."* The phrase is used in everyday situations, but it has its roots in military terms and literally means, "I am standing here at attention, waiting to hear what you will order me to do."

A military man knows that he must listen well to orders from a superior officer, and then he must obey or face the consequences. How can we be any less reverent to our great God?

How to Hear Him Better

What can we do to hear Him better? This is one of the most wonderful things about the ability to speak in tongues. It clears your mind and helps you to get ready to hear from God.

When I was a child, a neighbor of ours had a favorite saying. "I need to get my mind in neutral." At the time, I couldn't imagine what he meant by that, but in time I came to understand that he meant he needed to rid himself of all distractions so that he could focus on the matter at hand. That's what speaking in tongues will do for you. Get your mind cleared so that when God speaks, you can understand the direction He wants you to take.

"Here I am," Ananias said. He was ready to hear what God would say. If we complain that we're not hearing from God, it may be that He knows we're not listening, or He knows that we won't do what He tells us anyway, so He doesn't bother to tell us. If your mind is made up, why expect God to change it?

Some people say, "Well, I never hear from God. I don't understand those who say they are always hearing from Him. I never hear from Him." Maybe that person needs to examine himself to know why he never hears from God, for if we are willing to listen and willing to obey what He tells us, He will not fail to speak.

In Great Detail

Because Ananias was willing, God began to speak to him, and He spoke to him in great detail:

> *So the Lord said to him, "Arise and go to the street called Straight, and inquire at the house of Judas for one called Saul of Tarsus, for behold, he is praying. And in a vision he has seen a man named Ananias coming in and putting his hand on him, so that he might receive his sight."*
> Acts 9:11-12, NKJV

The detail of this is rather amazing. Ananias was to go to a certain street, to a certain house, owned by a certain man, and there he was to ask for someone named Saul. This man Saul was, at that very moment, praying and had seen a vision of Ananias himself coming in and laying his hands on him so that he could receive his sight. Wow!

There was a reason for all of this detail. God was sending Ananias to do something very dangerous. He would need to be able to say to himself and others: "The Lord spoke to me so clearly, so precisely, and with such detail that I cannot doubt it. He told me what street to go to. He told me what house to go to. He told me who owns the house. He told me the name of the man I am to see. And He said that the man was praying and had seen a vision of me coming in to lay hands on him."

Getting a message that specific helps us a lot. The reason is that other people tend to gainsay and cast doubt on the things we feel led to do for God. "Why on earth would you ever do such a thing?" they ask. If you can answer, "Because God told me the street, the house, the owner, the man's name, and everything else about it, so I know that this is God's will, and I must do it, I must go and lay my hands on him," that helps a lot.

A Man Needed His Help

In the vision Ananias received, there was a man who needed someone to help him, and that's what ministry is all about. We are not called to win fish or horses or dogs. It's people who need our help. This, we know, creates problems because people are so imperfect, so quirky, so unpredictable. And how do we get the people to whom we are sent to listen to us? That's a problem, but God was taking care of the problem.

This man Saul was desperate. Something so strange had happened to him on the road to Damascus that he would never be the same again. He had not eaten a bite of food in the past three days, and he was praying seriously, and now he, too, saw a vision. He saw a man coming in and laying hands on him, but it was not just any man. God identified the man in the vision as Ananias himself. This was important for both of them. It relieved Saul's mind about the one who would come, and it also opened the way for the ministry of Ananias.

When God sends you somewhere to minister to someone, He is not sending you on a little tourist jaunt. He has something special in mind. He knows that someone is hungering and thirsting for Him, and you are being sent in response to their earnest prayers. Because no one else has heard the cry, and no one else has heard God's heart in this situation, He is saying, "You be the one to go to that man, to bring him healing, to bring him the anointing of the Holy Spirit, and to bring him some divine guidance for his future."

God Works on Both Ends

It helps us that God is working on a given situation from both ends. On the one end, He is telling us what to do and why, and on the other end, He is telling the person or persons we will minister to who we are that are coming and why and what we will do when we get there.

God told Saul the man's name and showed him that when he came in and laid hands on him, he would be healed. Wow! That's the way God prepares things for us. So if you do your part, He will do His part, and when you get to the place He has told you to go, someone will be there waiting for you, ready to receive your ministry.

The people you are sent to may be in desperation. You may find them in tears. They may be at wits end. But one thing is sure: they will be hungry for God. That's why He has spoken to you to go. He promises:

Blessed are they which do hunger and thirst after righteousness: for they shall be filled.   Matthew 5:6

You're the answer to someone's prayers. Because they hungered, you are being called and sent.

The person or persons we are sent to might be on death's door. We don't know what their circumstance will be. What we know is that God is preparing us to go, and, at the same time, He is preparing those to whom we are being sent so that they will receive us. As we respond and carry the glory of God to them, their lives will be turned upside down. A Saul will become a Paul.

Ananias Had His Doubts

Ananias, like us, had his doubts. Even as God was speaking to him to do this amazing thing, he was remembering bad things he had heard about the man named Saul:

> *Then Ananias answered, "Lord, I have heard from many about this man, how much harm he has done to Your saints in Jerusalem. And here he has authority from the chief priests to bind all who call on Your name."*
> Acts 9:13-14, NKJV

The devil is always there, reminding us of any negative thing he can conjure up to cause us to disobey God. He uses fears, doubts, questionings, ponderings, gossip, or absolutely anything else he can. This time he was saying, "That man Saul is extremely dangerous. He kills Christians. Don't you dare go there. This is a trick. He is not the kind of man you want to get involved with. Nothing good can come of this."

Some of this may have been coming from Ananias' own mind, not just from the devil. Ananias knew too much about Saul. He had heard too much. He even knew the details, and it was all bad. His mind was agreeing with Satan, and he was so convinced that he argued with God. If he did this thing, his life would be in imminent danger. He would be putting his future at stake. Was that wise? Wanting to do the wise thing has kept many of us from obeying God.

Giving Away Their Children's Future

In January of 2014, we participated in the funeral of our long-time friend and ministry companion, Jack Chappell, in the Ashland Campground. On New Year's Day, at 84, he had gone out for his usual walk and run (which was always a time of prayer for him), and stepped over into the presence of God. When John and Pattie Chappell were being so generous with their money, giving to build every major building on the campground, giving to make possible the great crusade that kicked off the ministry the camp family had in Israel for many years, giving to many mission projects all over the world, and going themselves, they were severely criticized. People said things like, "They're giving away their children's future. What will become of those children?" Those who were privileged to attend the funeral heard from those children how proud they were of their father for having lived the life he did. Thank God he didn't listen to his critics.

Close Your Ears

When God speaks to you, close your ears to the naysayers around you. What they are saying is all lies, and they are nothing but tools of Satan. Some of them may be your most beloved family members, but Satan is using them. You love these people, and they love you, but they will still tell you the opposite of what God is saying. Close your ears. Get stubborn for God.

People will tell you, "What you are saying is the craziest thing I have ever heard. If you think you heard something from God, you need to think again." These may be wonderful people and in the future they might be a great blessing to you, but you cannot afford to listen to everyone's doubts, fears, and worries.

"But didn't you hear that _____ happened?" They will dream up anything to turn you aside.

Overcoming My Father's Objections

When I was called to take my first missionary trip that would include seventeen nations, my dad learned that one of them was India. He said, "Don't you know there are bandits in Bombay?" He must have seen an old movie at some time in the ancient past that portrayed bandits in Bombay, and that was enough reason for him to avoid it. Bombay, now Mumbai, proved to be wonderful, but to get there I had to overcome my father's objections.

Years later, when I was living in Ecuador, he knew that we were living by faith, so he wrote me a letter. In part, it said: "I'm very concerned about your children. Do they have the clothing they need and other essentials of life?" Soon after that our oldest daughter won the Best Dressed Award in her school, so I sent him a copy of the certificate.

All of those children attended great universities, mostly on great scholarships and finished with degrees in engineering, architecture, and communications. They are all doing well in their chosen professions and are active in their respective churches. God will do it for you, just as He did it for us and for the Chappell family.

The biblical story of Ananias doesn't mention other people's opinions, but there may well have been some. It would not be surprising if he had discussed the matter with other believers. They might have said, "You can't meet with that Saul fellow. You'll get us all killed. He's bad news. He is so full of the devil that he is killing Christians everywhere he goes. Please don't do this." What Ananias kept remembering was that he had heard God's voice, and God had told him what to do in such great detail. How could he question it? What God said finalized the matter:

What God Said Finalized the Matter

But the Lord said to him, "Go, for he is a chosen vessel of Mine to bear My name before Gentiles, kings, and the children of Israel. For I will show him how many things he must suffer for My name's sake."   Acts 9:15-16, NKJV

God didn't discount the things Ananias was saying, but His answer was: "Go anyway." Why? Because He had a great purpose for Saul's life. This man would do great things.

One of the greatest gifts needed in the ministry today is to be able to look at a person in all of their ungodliness and bad attitudes and see in them what God sees. He doesn't deal with us according to what we now are, but according to what we can become in Him. Oh, how we need that gift today!

The Heflins were amazing in this respect: they gave people opportunity when no one else would. Sometimes everyone else agreed that a certain person had no talent or ability at all, but at CPT they were given the opportunity to do something for God. There someone believed in them. This family had the gift of recognizing the potential of a seed.

Paul Accomplished It All

In time, Paul accomplished everything God said about him that day. He went to the Gentiles and established churches among them. He was even called the Apostle to the Gentiles. He witnessed before kings, both in the Middle East and at Rome. And he certainly was a great witness to his own people.

Paul had been a Pharisee of the Pharisees who hated Christians and persecuted them everywhere he could. Then, when he himself was changed, he made it his habit to go first to the synagogue of every city he entered to tell his own about Jesus. There is no way to calculate how many people Paul impacted in his lifetime, but it all started when a man from Damascus named Ananias was in prayer one day and heard from God.

Think About That

Now think about that. What do we know about Ananias? Not much. Was he the great Apostle Ananias? No.

Did he write many books? Not that we know of. Did he found great churches? Not that we know of.

This may not mean much. There were many thousands of people added to the Church in the first century. History shows that some of the early churches — like Ephesus, Thessalonica, and Corinth — had up to 15,000 members. Even the church at Jerusalem was large before the great persecution came. It was so large that they had no place to meet. They quickly outgrew the houses and other public meeting places. They were no longer welcome in the temple, so they met in what was called Solomon's Porches. It was a covered area beside the temple like an open-air porch. It was covered but not surrounded.

We know the detail of only a handful of those early believers, so maybe Ananias did more than we know about. We can't be sure. If Ananias wrote a book, it was not included in the Bible. So what did he do? Well, if nothing else, this one thing was powerful. One day he was praying, and God spoke to him to go and lay hands on a man who went on to forever change the history of the Church and the world. Ananias went:

"Ananias Went"

And Ananias went his way and entered the house; and laying his hands on him he said, "Brother Saul, the Lord Jesus, who appeared to you on the road as you came, has sent me that you may receive your sight and be filled with the Holy Spirit." Immediately there fell from his eyes something like scales, and he received his sight at once; and he arose and was baptized. Acts 9:17-18, NKJV

What did Ananias do? *"And Ananias went."* Did he seek counsel from some of his friends to see if he could get some confirmations? Today we want to get a large number of confirmations before we are willing to step out and obey God. Ananias just went.

Why do we know anything at all about Ananias? Because Ananias went. If there were naysayers, and there usually are, he ignored them. If there was contrary counsel, and that would not be at all surprising, he ignored it. He went, and because he went Saul was changed and went on to impact the world for God through all succeeding generations.

Yes, Ananias had to be praying. Yes, he had to be close enough to God to hear His voice. Yes, he had to be in the Spirit enough to see the vision. All of that was important. But if all of that had happened, but still he had not gone, nothing would have resulted. A vision is wonderful, but it is obedience to that vision that produces results for God's Kingdom.

"Servant of All"

Ananias went. This is what ministry is all about. It's not so that you can be elevated to lordship over a group that, then, does your bidding. Jesus clearly taught:

> *And whosoever of you will be the chiefest, shall be servant of all.*   Mark 10:44

Ananias was willing to be servant of all, and so he was sent to lay his hands on one who also would became servant of all.

Paul's Amazing Revelation

We must take a closer look at verse 16. To me this is one of the most amazing passages of the entire Bible. God said to Ananias (concerning Saul):

For I will show him how many things he must suffer for My name's sake.   Acts 9:15, NKJV

The King James Version of the Bible says it this way:

For I will shew him how great things he must suffer for my name's sake.

The Amplified Bible says:

For I will make clear to him how much he will be afflicted and must endure and suffer for My name's sake.

Wow! This was the revelation that came to Paul in Damascus. It was not how much his salary would be, how much his benefit package would be, or how much vacation time he would get. It was how much he would have to suffer for the sake of Christ.

An Integral Part of Paul's Ministry

Think about that. This was an integral part of Paul's call to the ministry. Three days earlier he had met Jesus on the road to Damascus. He was slain as that glorious light surrounded him, and he asked the Lord who He was. Jesus told him:

> *I am Jesus whom thou persecutest: it is hard for thee to kick against the pricks.*   Acts 9:5

Overwhelmed by the experience, Paul instinctively knew that this required something of him, and he asked what it was:

> *And he trembling and astonished said, Lord, what wilt thou have me to do?*   Acts 9:6

Jesus answered him:

> *Arise, and go into the city, and it shall be told thee what thou must do.*   Same Verse

Interestingly enough, the New Living Translation renders this passage a little differently. It says:

> *"Who are you, lord?" Saul asked.*
> *And the voice replied, "I am Jesus, the one you are persecuting! 6 Now get up and go into the city, and you will be told what you must do."*   Acts 9:5-6, NLT

WAS ANANIAS THE MESSENGER?

We can't be sure, but since God told Ananias that He would show Paul how much he would have to suffer for

Christ, it may well be that this was part of the message Ananias was to personally deliver to Paul that day. That would make sense.

Paul had already met Christ on the way into town, so he was now a believer, but Ananias ministered to him several important things: (1) He baptized Paul in water, (2) He ministered the Holy Spirit baptism to Paul, (3) He was the instrument used for Paul's healing from blindness, and (4) It seems very likely that he was used to relay to Paul some details of his calling and what it would require of him.

In this particular passage, it does not mention the details of Paul's sufferings. It just says *"I will show him how many things [how great things, KJV] he must suffer for My name's sake [how much he will be afflicted and must endure and suffer for My name's sake, AMP]."* We know the details from many other parts of Acts and from Paul's own words to the Corinthians:

> *In labors more abundant, in stripes above measure, in prisons more frequently, in deaths often. From the Jews five times I received forty stripes minus one. Three times I was beaten with rods; once I was stoned; three times I was shipwrecked; a night and a day I have been in the deep; in journeys often, in perils of waters, in perils of robbers, in perils of my own countrymen, in perils of the Gentiles, in perils in the city, in perils in the wilderness, in perils in the sea, in perils among false brethren; in weariness and toil, in sleeplessness often, in hunger and thirst, in fastings often, in cold*

and nakedness — besides the other things, what comes upon me daily: my deep concern for all the churches.
                              2 Corinthians 11:23-28, NKJV

If we are to understand God's words to Ananias, Paul would now learn all of this up front, before he had ever begun his ministry. This was his calling.

WHAT GOD DID NOT SAY

God definitely did not say to Ananias, "Go to Saul because I want to tell him how much I will pay him, how good his insurance will be, and what wonderful retirement benefits he can expect." The message of Ananias was not the bonus Paul could expect when he brought in new members and caused the church to grow. No! Instead, God said, "I want you to tell him how much he will suffer for My name's sake." I'm afraid that if the Lord spoke to us in this same way today, most of us would not be in the ministry at all.

Paul knew it all in advance. Later, when he was on his way to Jerusalem, and everyone was warning him that he was making a serious mistake and should not go on, his answer was that he already knew the dangers, but he had to go anyway. It may not have been "wisdom" in our eyes to go, but the Spirit compelled him to do it anyway. His work was not yet finished. He had to get to Jerusalem. He could not *not* go to Jerusalem. No wonder this man changed the world.

GET STUBBORN

This must become our attitude in ministry. Once you and I know the will of God, we must become stubborn and resist any efforts to turn us aside or turn us back. Refuse to listen to anyone else. Say, "I cannot *not* do what God has told me to do."

God told Ananias, "Go," and "Ananias went." When he got to the place God had indicated, the right street and the right house, there he encountered the man God had told him about, and what God told him would happen did happen. It was all very miraculous, and we need the miraculous to show us that we're on the right road.

Ananias had the ideal mentality for this ministry. He was not concerned for his own life, but became willing to obey the Lord, whatever the cost. This brings to mind the attitude of the original disciples.

THE BLIND OBEDIENCE OF THE DISCIPLES

When Jesus encountered Simon Peter and Andrew fishing along the shores of the Sea of Galilee, He called them:

And Jesus, walking by the Sea of Galilee, saw two brothers, Simon called Peter, and Andrew his brother, casting a net into the sea; for they were fishermen. Then He said to them, "Follow Me, and I will make you fishers of men."
                    Matthew 4:18-19, NKJV

And what was their response?

They immediately left their nets and followed Him.
                                    Matthew 4:20, NKJV

Wow!

Next, Jesus encountered two more brothers. These were mending their nets:

Going on from there, He saw two other brothers, James the son of Zebedee, and John his brother, in the boat with Zebedee their father, mending their nets. He called them.
                                    Matthew 4:21, NKJV

And what was their response?

And immediately they left the boat and their father, and followed Him.   Matthew 4:22, NKJV

Wow! That almost sounds irresponsible, doesn't it? Those boats and those nets were valuable assets. Should they just leave them like that? Well, the secret is to do whatever the Lord says to do. Whatever it takes, that is what is required of us.

JACK'S EASY LIFE WAS INTERRUPTED

In the case of Jack Chappell, he inherited an insurance firm from his father and only had to go to the office a couple hours a day. The rest of the time he could play tennis. He told me that his greatest trial came one day when the air-conditioning went out on his Cadillac. He and Pattie had a beautiful home on a lovely street in Richmond, and the future looked bright. Then the Lord called them to missionary life.

Their response was to sell their home, eventually sell their business, and to go to the Philippines to live with their four children in two small rooms in a house we had rented there. They went, and the rest is history.

When He says "Go," We Need to Go

If you don't go, what can God do? His hands are tied.

Will we dare to blame God because nothing has been accomplished? When He says, "Go," we need to act. That's what Ananias did, and we see the fruits of his obedience.

Serving Undesirables

Ananias became willing to serve someone who was not considered to be a nice person. He had heard the stories of Saul's treachery. We now know that Saul had changed, but no one else knew that yet. Everything they knew about the man was bad. The man was vicious. He was killing Christians, men and women alike. He must have had a demon or perhaps many demons in him. Who would want to risk trying to help such a man? Most of us would not have wanted to get anywhere near him. But those most difficult cases are the ones God delights in saving, and He is glorified in the process, and others are convinced of His goodness.

In the early 1960s, when I was still very young, I was preaching a series of meetings in a town in central India. Among those who came to the altar for prayer one night was a certain lady. I could not have known her from any of the others, but the rest of the people there knew her reputation. She was a woman of the streets. When I got to her and began praying, the pastor came behind me and gently guided me to someone else he deemed more suitable for prayer. I asked him why, and he said, "She's a bad woman." I never forgot that, and it bothered me a lot. Isn't that the kind of people who need our prayers? We should want to go to the worst of the worst and help to lift them up.

This is our calling. The righteous don't need us nearly as much. Jesus said:

They that are whole have no need of the physician, but they that are sick: I came not to call the righteous, but sinners to repentance. Mark 2:17

I Honor the Memory of Ananias

I honor the memory of Ananias today. Although I don't know much about him, I know that he was a great man of God. We will one day meet him in Heaven and can then say, "So you're the man who got the great Paul started in ministry. You're the one who went boldly to lay hands on him. You're the one who shared that initial vision with him." And we'll be thrilled to shake the man's hand. Through the humility and obedience of

Ananias, Saul received a spirit of serving that took him to the nations.

I've been in churches where they sit their pastor on a beautiful throne. Then everyone comes in and bows before him and kisses his gorgeous ring. It shocked me.

I've known ministers who were very happy to have finally gathered a little group together, because these people could now wait on him hand and foot. I've overheard them saying, "You, come here. I have something I need you to do for me. You, over there, come here. Yes, you, go get me a …" Jesus said that if we want to be the greatest of all, we must first become the servant of all.

Ananias went because he was the servant of all, and Paul, too, became the servant of all. His first revelation was not of the greatness he would achieve in life, but, rather, of the greatness of his sufferings for Christ. It was not how well he would be known because of writing so much of the Bible. It was not how the Gentile churches would honor him because he was their father in the faith or because he was used by God to raise up elders to lead them forward. It was not because of the many younger men who would travel with him, learn from him, and then have ministries of their own. His first great revelation was of trials and tests, opposition, and imprisonment.

Paul Was Not Discouraged

Paul could have become discouraged in that moment, and maybe some of us would have. I can't say what I would have done. I don't know. But when we look at ministry from the aspect of privilege and never as a sacrifice, it's altogether different.

That's what Paul did. He had met someone so powerful that he was struck to the ground and lost his sight. Now, three days later, the scales fell from his eyes, he was filled with the Spirit, and baptized in water. And what does the final verses of the passage say:

> *So when he had received food, he was strengthened. Then Saul spent some days with the disciples at Damascus. Immediately he preached the Christ in the synagogues, that He is the Son of God.* Acts 9:19-20, NKJV

Paul did not allow many days to pass before he began preaching, and he did it in the most dangerous place possible. He had come there to Damascus to work with the people of the synagogue to rid the town of Christians, and now he was one of them. Still, *"Immediately he preached,"* and he kept on preaching, and many times through the years he retold the story of what had happened to him there in Damascus. It was life-changing, and it happened through a humble man called Ananias.

PAUL NEVER TIRED OF TELLING THE STORY

This was the foundation of Paul's Christian life and ministry, and so he never tired of telling the story. "There was a man named Ananias. One day, as he was praying, God told him to come to the house where I was being kept and lay his hands on me. He came, and when he put those hands on me, wonderful things happened.

"I knew that something wonderful was going to happen because I had seen this man in a vision. No sooner were his hands laid on me than something like scales fell from my eyes, and I could see again. How I rejoiced that day! And I've never stopped rejoicing since."

What About You?

What about you? Would you let God use you to impact some of our modern-day Sauls? There are people in prayer this minute, desperately waiting for someone to come help them. Will you go?

When we sent out Filipino missionaries to other countries, we purposely did not give them a single address to contact. We wanted them to pray and find those who were waiting for them to come. One of the first groups went to Taiwan. They prayed for a few hours there in the Taipei airport. Then they got a taxi and made hand signals to the driver to take them down one street and then another until they felt led to stop. When they knocked on a door, they found a group of Presbyterian believers inside on their knees asking God to send them revival. They not only received the power of the Holy Spirit, but they then took the team across that island ministering in many places. This happened again and again.

Understanding the Seed
It Happened to Me

I could send those Filipino young people to other countries with no contacts because I had experienced it. It happened to me.

I was ministering in Indonesia in 1964. That was the same year I had met Sister Ruth Heflin in India (in January). I also met Sister Gwen Shaw in Java in June, and we did some conferences together. Now I was on the island of Bali working with a wonderful New Zealand missionary.

I loved Bali because it was so spiritually needy. It was the only Hindu part of Indonesia. I worked well with the missionary as my interpreter, and I especially loved speaking to the students of his Bible school, but also in evangelistic meetings around the area. Then one day, the Lord spoke to me very clearly and said, "Go to Singapore on August the 16th."

When I told my host what the Lord had said, he said to me, "Oh, my goodness, you can't go to Singapore." He explained that Singapore was then part of Malaysia and that the Prime Minister of Malaysia and the President of Indonesia didn't like each other, and so the two countries were at war. All contact — phone service, cable service, and even mail service — had been suspended.

"Who do you know in Singapore?" he asked me.

I had to admit that I didn't know anyone there.

"Then where would you go and what would you do?" he asked.

I didn't have an answer for that. I didn't know.

He was very excited about a crusade he had set up for the two of us in the mountains of Bali. The people there were also excited, and he hated to disappoint them. He pleaded with me to stay.

I was young and impressionable, and everything the man said made perfect sense to me. Since I didn't know anyone in Singapore, there was no communication, and I wouldn't know where to go or what to do, maybe I should just stay where I was being useful. After all, Bali was very beautiful, and many people there needed God, so I relented and stayed.

Riots Broke Out

On August 16, riots broke out all over Indonesia against the United States. The U.S. Library in Jogjakarta was burned. Before long a policeman knocked on the door and told the missionary that he must keep me off of the streets of Bali. It was not safe for an American right then. I was suddenly grounded.

There was still some hope that we could travel to that mountain place and do the planned crusade. Next the missionary mysteriously lost his voice. There was nothing to explain it. He wasn't sick. He hadn't abused his voice. It just went, and all he could manage was a whisper. He apologized, saying that there was no way we could now do that mountain crusade. I went to my room and prayed and was led to pack my bag and go to the airport, hoping to get the first flight out to Djakarta.

UNDERSTANDING THE SEED

No Hope?

At the airport, I was told that there was absolutely no hope of me getting on a flight to Djakarta. Because of the riots, the military was mobilizing, and all empty seats were reserved for them. This would be true for days to come. I should go back and stay.

I told the agent that I would be on the next flight to Djakarta and that I would be waiting nearby for his call. He scoffed at that, but I waited. I don't remember how long I waited. It didn't matter. I was going to Djakarta. It was the only city that had connections to Singapore, and I was going to Singapore.

Eventually someone came and told me that there was one unexpected seat open and that if I wanted to be on the plane I needed to run. Its engines were already warming up. I ran. Once in Djakarta, I never left the airport. I caught the next flight out to Singapore.

Arriving in Singapore

When I got to the airport in Singapore, there were many taxis lined up. The drivers asked me where I was going. I told them I didn't know. They asked me if someone was coming to pick me up. I said I didn't think so. When nothing else materialized I decided to find a YMCA and spend a few days in fasting and prayer. I had enough money for that. (If I remember right, the room cost me $3.00 a night.)

After three days of fasting and prayer, I suddenly remembered a name an Indian pastor had mentioned to me six months before. I've always been terrible with names, and often forget immediately what someone has told me. He told me he had a brother-in-law in ministry somewhere in Singapore and told me his name. I now set out to find that brother-in-law.

A City of Millions

Even then Singapore was a city of millions, and there were lots of Indians in Singapore. There were some Indian churches and Indian pastors. I now went from place to place telling people that God had sent me to Singapore. I didn't know who I was to see or what I was to do. Could they help me? Believe it or not, eventually I found the place where that man had been pastoring. The bad news was that he had gone back to India. So … now what was I to do?

They told me they knew another Indian pastor who might be able to help me. I agreed to meet him the next day. I met the pastor. He was a very sweet man, but he wasn't sure he could help me. He invited me to speak in his church on Sunday, but he didn't have other activities planned.

After we had talked for a while, he told me to come back the next afternoon. He wanted to take me to meet a friend of his, a Finnish missionary. He thought the man just might be able to help me.

Meeting the Finnish Missionary

I came back the next day, and being young and unwise, I came wearing a red short-sleeved sport shirt. It was something I usually just relaxed in during the day, and since it was hot in Singapore that day, I had left it on.

We came to the home of the Finnish missionary, and as we were being shown in the gate, the wife appeared in an upper window and began rejoicing about something. I wasn't sure what. I was introduced, she served us something to drink, and said that her husband would be there soon. She seemed awfully happy about something.

Within a half hour or so, the husband arrived. He was out of breath and was rushing about, but, he too seemed awfully happy about something. He apologized for not having more time to spend with us and then quickly ran off to wash his hands. In a few moments he was back, shook hands formally, and began to explain.

He had just come from the crusade sight. He had just gotten the finishing touches on the tent, the folding chairs, and the musical instruments. Still breathless and very joyful, He told us: "I am not an evangelist, ... more of an administrator. Some months ago, the Lord told me that if I would bring a tent out from Finland and make all the preparations, He would send the preacher. The advertising has gone out, the crusade sight is all ready. You're the preacher God has sent.

We didn't have time to digest all of this because now he said, "Now, we must go because the meeting will begin in thirty minutes." I borrowed a Bible from him and preached the first night of that wonderful week-long crusade in my red short-sleeved sport shirt. God did some wonderful things.

Meeting Goh Ewe Kheng

That first night I had a long line of people to pray for, those who wanted to be saved and those who wanted to be healed. It took quite some time to minister to them all.

I noticed a man who had been standing at the front the entire time. He was a Chinese man, but other than that, there was nothing very noticeable about him, except that he seemed to be very humble. He had stood there the whole time, with his arms folded humbly, waiting patiently for me to finish.

Now that there was no one else waiting to be prayed for, he looked up at me warmly. I approached him, and he told me who he was: Goh Ewe Kheng, with the Church of Singapore. He asked where I was staying, and I told him the Y. "Well, the Lord told me to take you to my house," he said. I'll be coming by tomorrow morning to pick you up.

The next morning, he was there a little earlier than he had told me, and while I was gathering up a few things and putting them in my suitcase, he paid my bill downstairs. I went to the desk to turn in my key and take care of the bill, and found that it was already taken care of.

An Amazing Man

On the way to his house, I learned a lot about Goh Ewe Kheng, but I had to pull it all out of him. He was not a boastful man. As it turned out, aside from being an elder at his church, he was a very wealthy businessman. He owned the lucrative Yashica camera franchise for all of Malaysia, and he had a factory that made a local brand of toothpaste, soap, and many other common personal items.

As we approached his house, he said to me, "There are several vehicles here, and each one has its driver. If you need to go anywhere, just tell one of them, and they'll take you wherever you need to go."

I was in Singapore for many weeks to come, and it was a busy time. Then Brother Goh arranged special meetings for me in five of Malaysia's largest cities. He paid all of the expenses. He bought my air tickets, accompanied me, and was my interpreter in each place.

When we were back in Singapore, many evenings, when I came back to my room, there was a gift on my bed. By now I had been away from home for ten months, and because I was traveling light, some of my clothes were becoming worn. Now I had new pajamas, new under garments, a new shirt, a hand-tailored suit, a new 35 mm camera.

In the years to come, Goh Ewe Kheng sponsored the printing of my first two books and shipped them all over the world. During the time I was in the Philippines, he sent us movie projectors, amplifying equipment, camera equipment, and more. In later years, he helped me get musical instruments for the ministry in several Asian countries. How glad I was that I had gone to Singapore as the Lord had shown me. We cannot lose when we obey His voice. Will you hear God's call today?

Amen!

Chapter 3

Understanding the Seed, Part I
by Pastor Peter Kange

If you are in ministry, that is wonderful. As ministers, we need to hear from God and receive His touch so that we can pass it along to others. God wants us to be changed first so that we can then help others change.

It has been said that doctors make the worst patients, and I somehow believe that ministers make the worst students. We sometimes feel that we are too busy to sit and learn. We get so busy that we think we don't even have time to seek God. But if we don't meet with God, how can we have something worthwhile to feed to others? If we are not willing to change, how can we expect those to whom we minister to change?

Did you ever notice in a worship service that often it is the ministers who are not worshipping? If we are not first worshippers of God, what can we hope to receive from Him and pass along to others? Ministry is giving out what we have received. If we have not received, what can we hope to give? We must first be partakers of God's goodness before we can minister that goodness to others. We cannot give what we don't have.

When it is time to worship, we ministers need to be worshipping. When it is time to give, we need to be giving. When it is time to learn from the Word, we need to be learning from the Word. We can effectively challenge others spiritually only to the extent that we have been challenged ourselves.

We are not too spiritual to worship, too spiritual to seek the face of God, or too spiritual to learn from the Word. Be real, meaning be honest and sincere with God and yourself, and begin to flow with what He is doing at the moment, and He will prepare you to be used in a greater way for His glory.

The Importance of Praying in the Holy Ghost

One of the things all ministers need more of is time praying in the Holy Ghost. It is shameful to have to say it, but many ministers have actually abandoned their prayer life. That's not right. How can we represent God if we don't even spend time talking to Him and listening to Him? Have you stopped raising your hands to God? Have you stopped praising His name? Have you stopped speaking in tongues? Many have. If you are one of them, then you need a refreshing from on high.

We are called to be church leaders, the people whom God is releasing to make a difference in the world. We are to be the ones building others up, so that they, too, can do the work of the ministry. Therefore, we must first come to God and build ourselves up on our most holy faith, praying in the Spirit.

Building Yourself Up

Are you tired of walking in the sensual realm and want to live in the Spirit? Then pray in the Holy Ghost. As you pray in the Spirit, you are not only building yourself up in your holy faith; you are also sharpening your inner man, your spirit man, to hear the voice of God from another realm.

As you pray in the Holy Ghost, accessing that other realm, keep ascending until you sense a breaking forth in your inner man. Keep ascending, for you are positioning yourself for a miracle. You are positioning yourself for a shift.

As you pray, you are not binding any demon, and you are not asking for anything specific from God. You are simply waiting on Him in the Spirit, communing with Him as with a lover. In this way, you are building yourself up in your most holy faith, but you are also speaking mysteries unto God. The more you pray in the Spirit, the more you are telling the Lord, "I am ready to hear You. Speak to me." This is a position of revival.

Revival of Positioning

Revival not only depends on being in the right place at the right time; it requires that you get in the Spirit. Then, as you pray in the Holy Ghost, a shift is taking place. You are being properly positioned by the Spirit of God, and miracles will follow.

Each of us wrestles with certain character issues that we seem unable to overcome. All ministers are nothing more than redeemed men and women. As we take time to pray in the Spirit, such issues are suddenly broken loose from us, and we begin to ascend to a new level. A major shift takes place in our spirits.

As this is happening, give all the glory to Jesus. Let Him know that you realize and appreciate the wonderful things He is doing for you. Worship Him. Magnify Him. Lift up His name. Be first ministers to God, so that you can be His ministers to others.

Be an Example

When another person is ministering, you need to set an example by being the most attentive person in the room. Listen, really listen, to what the Holy Ghost is saying.

Most people, when they stand to minister to others, are speaking from the experience of having lived the very thing they are now preaching to others. The thing they are teaching has already worked in their lives. They have been touched by the Lord in that area, and this qualifies them to speak to others from that place of experience. This, at least, is how it should be.

Personally, I never get tired of finding awesome and amazing things in the Word of God. Not long ago, for instance, I was reading the Scriptures in Luke 4, where Jesus was going into the synagogue in His hometown of Nazareth, and verse 16 says this was *"as his custom was."* So this is what He had always done from the time He was a child. It had become His regular custom, or habit.

The next thing I noticed was in verse 17. It said, *"He found the place where it was written ...,"* and the familiar passage we all know followed, beginning with those powerful words, *"The Spirit of the Lord is upon me"* (verse 18). You don't find something unless you are looking for it. Jesus was seeking, and that's why He found what He was looking for.

The Holy Ghost knew what He was doing that day, and He had put that scripture there for a reason. What Jesus was reading about had come to town, and Jesus was able to declare, *"This day is this scripture fulfilled in your ears"* (verse 21). What am I saying? If you will seek God, you, too, will find.

Making It Happen

I am about to share something with you, and I need for you to follow me carefully so that you get the fullness of it. It relates to all of the prophetic words that have gone forth over your life in days gone by and whether or not they will come to pass. Will they manifest themselves? Or will they remain unfulfilled words?

Nothing in the Kingdom of God just happens. You have to work at it. If you are willing, let God speak to you through this chapter. He is a miracle-working God.

Late last year a pastor came to visit me in my office and asked if he could use our sanctuary for a special service of thanksgiving with his family. Although we had never allowed our sanctuary to be used by other groups, I was led to grant his petition. So, on New Year's Day, his family was gathered in our sanctuary.

I attended their service, and after their prayers of thanksgiving, they asked me to come forward and pray for their family. I gave them several testimonies of things God had recently done in our family and then I prayed for them.

I had noticed a lady in her seventies sitting to one side in a wheelchair, and now I went over to her and prayed, and she got up and began walking. I loved her testimony. She began by saying, "Something is moving in my body, my knees, my legs." And then she literally jumped out of the wheelchair and ran.

A similar thing happened in another service. I noticed a crippled man coming in during praise and worship, and I also saw an angel going in his direction. I was playing the keyboard at the time, but I stopped and watched to see where the angel would go. The angel went right to that crippled man, and God said to me, "This man will walk today."

I said, "Really? Well, then let's get him walking."

I went to him and told him what God had said. I told him to start walking, and he walked.

While he was walking, I realized that one of his legs was shorter than the other. I had him sit down on the platform and I held his two legs side by side. It was evident to all that one was shorter. Now the whole church ran to the front to see what would happen. We prayed, and his short leg grew out.

Understanding the Seed, Part I

I am noticing that God is doing miracles in spite of us. Every miracle is an act of God. It has nothing to do with our voice or our hands. It has nothing to do with us — period. So when God says, *"They shall lay hands on the sick, and they shall recover,"* (Mark 16:18), we should say to the sick, "Okay, recover." It's just that easy. Praise God.

The Potential of the Seed

Now, for the lesson I want to give you in this chapter, I want you to find a grain of corn (popcorn will do) and hold it in your hand. There's an important reason for this. That grain has a deep meaning. Examine it well, and hold onto it. By the time you have finished reading this book, you'll understand my reasons and it will be very meaningful to you.

Now let's read from Mark 4:

> *¹ And he began again to teach by the sea side: and there was gathered unto him a great multitude, so that he entered into a ship, and sat in the sea; and the whole multitude was by the sea on the land.*
> *² And he taught them many things by parables, and said unto them in his doctrine,*
> *³ Hearken; Behold, there went out a sower to sow:*
> *⁴ And it came to pass, as he sowed, some fell by the way side, and the fowls of the air came and devoured it up.*
> *⁵ And some fell on stony ground, where it had not much*

earth; and immediately it sprang up, because it had no depth of earth:
⁶ But when the sun was up, it was scorched; and because it had no root, it withered away.
⁷ And some fell among thorns, and the thorns grew up, and choked it, and it yielded no fruit.
⁸ And other fell on good ground, and did yield fruit that sprang up and increased; and brought forth, some thirty, and some sixty, and some an hundred.

Do you see the progressive nature of this parable? It does not start by talking about fruit, but it ends up talking about fruit. It begins first by talking about the sower, then the seed, then the ground, and then the fruit.

Jesus continued:

⁹ And he said unto them, He that hath ears to hear, let him hear.
¹⁰ And when he was alone, they that were about him with the twelve asked of him the parable.
¹¹ And he said unto them, Unto you it is given to know the mystery of the kingdom of God: but unto them that are without, all these things are done in parables.

When the Word says, "Unto you it is given to know," this does not mean simply to be informed. Rather, it means, "Unto you it is given to practicalize, or put into practice." The use of this word *mysteries* means that it is complex and many sided. So if you look at it from one angle only, you might miss a lot.

Understanding the Seed, Part I

Up to now, I know that what I am saying are things that almost every minister understands, but stick with me. I'm going somewhere with this. Please stay in the Spirit and flow with me as you read.

Now, let's look at verse 11 again:

¹¹ And he said unto them, Unto you it is given to know the mystery of the kingdom of God: but unto them that are without, all these things are done in parables.

Now take note of verse 14:

¹⁴ The sower soweth the word.

Just before this, however, Jesus had asked the important question:

Know ye not this parable? and how then will ye know all parables?   Mark 4:13

Clearly this teaching is important. It holds the key to all parables. Remembering that the idea of all the parables was to reveal truths about God's Kingdom, now we see that if we do not understand this particular parable, we will be totally lacking in understanding concerning them all. That being the case, how could we then expect to walk in the mysteries of the Kingdom of God?

Understanding the Seed

Following the Progression

As we noted earlier, this parable is progressive. Now, let's follow it some more and see where that progression takes us.

Verse 14, again, pronounces the truth that the sower sows the Word. This indicates that the Word is a seed, and the seed we are contemplating is the Word.

What else do we learn?

> *¹⁵ And these are they by the way side, where the word is sown; but when they have heard, Satan cometh immediately, and taketh away the word that was sown in their hearts.*
> *¹⁶ And these are they likewise which are sown on stony ground; who, when they have heard the word, immediately receive it with gladness;*
> *¹⁷ And have no root in themselves, and so endure but for a time: afterward, when affliction or persecution ariseth for the word's sake, immediately they are offended.*

When we started, what did we say the seed was? It was the Word, and we read about that Word being sown on the way side. What, then, is the very next verse saying, when it declares, *"And these are they likewise which are sown on stony ground?"*

Please take another look at this passage. Who are the *"they"* referred to here as being sown in the ground? *They* are clearly not words. We have somehow moved from a seed, which is the Word of God, and now we are talking about *people* as seeds.

How did we move from seeds being sown to people being sown? You may not have heard this before, but that is okay. Take a look at it one more time. Do you see it now?

Who has no root in them? The people who are sown. What was sown originally? The Word. Does the Word have to hear the Word? So why are we told that the Word was sown, and then it goes on to say, in verse 16, *"When they have heard the word ... ?"* Why does it say, in verse 17, *"When affliction or persecution ariseth for the word's sake, immediately they are offended?"* Can the Word be offended? Or is it people who are offended?

The sower went out to sow the Word, the seed, people. The seed, the people, were sown on some kind of soil or territory, and when they were sown in this soil or territory, various things began to happen, based on how they were able to respond to that kind of soil or territory.

This cannot be referring to God's Word. Do you believe that the Word of God yields completely or only partially? It does not yield just portions. If it yields only portions, then there is a problem with God, and there is no problem with God. He is all righteous, all just, all knowing, everything to the max, all sufficient, and all powerful. If His power is in portions, there is a problem. So that cannot happen. Yet this parable is clearly progressive.

Do we all agree that the seed is the Word? Yes. But then, as we progress in the parable, do we have other elements showing up? Yes, we do.

You Are What Has Been Spoken Over You

Now let me ask you a question: When you think of Moses, what comes to your mind? Probably the exodus and the fact that he became a deliverer. And why does that come to our minds? Because that was the word of the Lord concerning Moses.

When you hear the name Jesus or Emmanuel, what comes to you? Probably this: *"And she shall bring forth a son, and thou shalt call his name Jesus: for he shall save his people from their sins"* (Matthew 1:21). That is what God's Word declared over Jesus.

When you hear the name John the Baptist, what comes to mind? He was the forerunner who prepared the way for the coming of Jesus. That was exactly what the Word of God declared over him.

Now, when I hear your name, what should come to my mind? In the same way, it should be the word that has been spoken concerning your life. Let us begin to see each other as God sees us.

The Mystery of the Seed

When we don't rush over these verses of Mark 4, this is what we see: the word is spoken to a vessel, that vessel becomes the carrier of that word, and the sower who sowed the word into this vessel takes the vessel and sows it in a certain soil or territory.

And what does it all mean? Scripture explains scripture, so let's look at some other passages that deal with the seed:

Understanding the Seed, Part I

In Genesis 12, God appeared to Abraham and said to him:

Unto thy seed will I give this land: and there builded he an altar unto the Lord, who appeared unto him.
Genesis 12:7

In Genesis 3, we find a mystery regarding the seed. The seed was to somehow overcome the devil (see verse 15). Keep in mind that when it comes to the Kingdom of God, we must recognize any seed that comes from the hand of God Himself.

Why should any of this matter to us? Because God is working on all of us, and He has been telling us that we will come to the place that there will no longer be any failures in our personal lives and ministries. Some of us have been in ministry for a long time now, but we are about to experience an explosion in ministry. Increase is coming to you and me. Abundance is coming in the work of God. There will be miracles, signs, and wonders happening on a new level in the days ahead.

Isaiah and the Seed

Isaiah also spoke of the seed:

Isaiah 55:6-11
⁶ Seek ye the Lord while he may be found, call ye upon him while he is near:
⁷ Let the wicked forsake his way, and the unrighteous man his thoughts: and let him return unto the Lord, and he

will have mercy upon him; and to our God, for he will abundantly pardon.

⁸ For my thoughts are not your thoughts, neither are your ways my ways, saith the LORD.

⁹ For as the heavens are higher than the earth, so are my ways higher than your ways, and my thoughts than your thoughts.

¹⁰ For as the rain cometh down, and the snow from heaven, and returneth not thither, but watereth the earth, and maketh it bring forth and bud, that it may give seed to the sower, and bread to the eater:

¹¹ So shall my word be that goeth forth out of my mouth: it shall not return unto me void, but it shall accomplish that which I please, and it shall prosper in the thing whereto I sent it.

Who should seek the Lord? You should seek the Lord, and I should seek the Lord. Why? So that we can know His thoughts and His ways. If He can change our thoughts, then He can change our ways too.

What is God talking about in this passage? Is it about the Word? Or is it about the person who should seek the Lord? I hope you see here that you are to be the bearer of the Word of God and that He promises that if you will be, you will prosper in the thing whereto He has sent you.

In this passage, God is saying to you, "My thoughts are higher than your thoughts." Why is this needful? Because you have been thinking, *"I don't know how this thing will work."* You have actually said to God, "You should use someone else." God is taking issue with your carnal thoughts and calling on you to abandon them and adopt His thoughts.

God says, *"My thoughts are higher than your thoughts; My ways are higher than your ways."* Your thoughts are producing your ways, but if you will yield to God's thoughts, then you will also have His ways.

Here God likens a word from Him to rain. Rain falls and does its job, before its water eventually goes back up into the clouds. And if you will yield to the word God has given you, then you, too, will accomplish what you were intended to accomplish. You will not fail. Trust God for it. He said:

> *Not by might, nor by power, but by my spirit, saith the Lord of hosts.*   Zechariah 4:6

That is His instruction for you, and if you follow it, you will accomplish His intent.

What Is Prosperity?

The thing you must be careful about is what you consider to be prosperity. If you are doing what you are supposed to do, on instruction from the Lord, even if it is ministering to a single person, He will cause you to prosper. We don't always have to have a crowd, but we do have to do our part. We are to prosper in the thing whereto He has sent *us* — whatever it happens to be.

Why do you think you are so persistent? Is it because that is your nature? If it were up to you, you would have quit a long time ago. But something about God's word to you and in you is making you stick it out, despite everything that has come against you.

It's one thing to be a pastor, but it's another thing to be a parent. Both words (seeds) have been spoken over me. I have signed up to be a parent, because God has placed the substance of the seed within me. My prosperity in ministry is, therefore, dependent upon me walking in the awareness of that word, which requires me to parent those I have been called to pastor.

"Ye Shall Go Out with Joy"

Isaiah continued:

For ye shall go out with joy, and be led forth with peace: the mountains and the hills shall break forth before you into singing, and all the trees of the field shall clap their hands.   Isaiah 55:12

Who shall go out with joy? The one who was seeking the face of the Lord in verse 6. You shall go out with joy because you are a spoken word. You have heard from God. He said: *"They shall lay hands on the sick, and they shall recover"* (Mark 16:18), so you can go out with joy, knowing that you will prosper in the thing that you have been sent to do.

It's time to send the devil some bad news. You can preach again, and souls will be blessed. You can lay hands on the sick again, and they will recover. For a time, the devil seemed to block your thoughts, but now you are hearing God afresh and anew. So you are scheduled to prosper. You are on schedule to increase.

The One who sends you is also the One who empowers you. He infuses strength into you. Even if you do not feel it, His strength is within you. You just need to yield to it, in order to prosper in the thing whereto He has sent you.

SCHEDULED TO PROSPER

You're on schedule to prosper. That is the reason God said, in Isaiah 60:1:

> *Arise [from the depression and prostration in which circumstances have kept you — rise to a new life]! Shine (be radiant with the glory of the Lord), for your light has come, and the glory of the Lord has risen upon you!* (AMP)

Our God not only calls us to arise from our depression; He is also calling us to arise above the voices around us that tell us that we cannot make it. Some of you have been hearing such voices for months or even years, but you are still around. The fact that you are still around is proof that you are prospering against the voices predicting your demise. You will prosper because you have been prosperous until now.

EVERYTHING IN THE SEED REMAINS INTACT

The Lord has been reminding me that no matter how cold it gets outside, everything that is in a seed remains intact. It does not matter what the weather happens to be like. A seed will not die. You also are not dying before your time, and that is not because you are so very prayerful; it is because you are a seed and a seed does not die.

Seed ... Child... Children

Throughout the Word of God, we find the words *seed*, *child*, and *children* being used interchangeably:

I and the children the Lord has given me are for signs and for wonders.   Isaiah 8:18

Genesis 8:22 declares:

While the earth remains, seedtime and harvest, cold and heat, summer and winter, and day and night shall not cease.

With this, I really want to talk to the voice that has been telling you many wrong things. As long as the earth remains, it will be your time (seed time, for you are the seed), and so your harvest time is coming.

Please don't be a conditional Christian. When the sun is up, they are mighty prayer warriors, but when it goes down, they stop praying entirely. Don't live your life like that. You are the seed of God. Be fervent always. The seed does not change.

You Become the Seed

Let's think of someone we know. If the Lord speaks to that person, releasing a seed in them and they allow it to

Understanding the Seed, Part I

grow, they become that seed. Their thoughts become the thoughts of the seed, which are the thoughts of the Father. Their ways become the ways of the seed, which are the ways of the Father. The Father has changed that person's ways because of the seed, and this shows us that the seed is doing its work. It is seeding. God's ways are seed ways, and when His seed grows in us, our ways become seed ways too.

Actions vs. Ways

Now, let's substitute *actions* for *ways*. Everything this person now does is a seed action. When they go to another person and perform a seed action — an expression of love — what happens? A new seed is sown. And what is the response? That new person now becomes the seed also.

Let's take some scriptural examples and see how this becomes a practical matter:

> *A man that hath friends must shew himself friendly: and there is a friend that sticketh closer than a brother.*
> Proverbs 18:24

> *Be not deceived; God is not mocked: for whatsoever a man soweth, that shall he also reap.*   Galatians 6:7

Everything that you do is a seed action, and you will reap from all of your seed actions.

God has said, *"They shall lay hands on the sick, and they shall recover,"* (Mark 16:18). If your thoughts are transformed by that word, you will begin to behave like the seed that has been planted in you. Then, when you lay hands on the sick, you are seeding, and there will be a harvest.

Don't worry about the English. I know it should be sowing, but I want to make a point here. You get seeded, and then, when you seed others, what happens? As long as earth remains, when you do the seeding, you will receive the corresponding harvest.

Seed Actions

If you are dressed today, you most probably dressed yourself. As you put on those clothes, you were sowing seeds, or seeding. You knew you needed to be clothed, so you acted accordingly. You did whatever was necessary to put each item of clothing on. For each of those items, you produced a seed action, and the end result was that you are now fully clothed.

If you want to go somewhere, you must produce some seed action that makes it possible. Will you drive? Ride a bus? Walk? If you expect the harvest of arriving at your desired destination, you must produce whatever seed action is necessary to make it happen. Every harvest is a product of your seed actions.

Satan Has His Own Mission

The devil, of course, reminds us of our evil harvests. That's his work. The Scriptures reveal his tactics:

Understanding the Seed, Part I

And these are they by the way side, where the word is sown; but when they have heard, Satan cometh immediately, and taketh away the word that was sown in their hearts. Mark 4:15

Satan is persistent and faithful to his task, but since we know he is coming, we can prepare ourselves so that he will not have an effective ministry in us.

Satan has his own mission, and he sows his own seeds. In fact, he is a master at seeding and getting us to seed negatively into others. We become depressed because we have sown a seed to be depressed. How do we do that? By not rejecting the seed suggestions someone has offered us. The seed we sow in that moment should be "No!" And when we sow "No," what do we get? We get no depression because we have said, "No!" It is then that we can *"go out with joy"* (Isaiah 55:12) because we refused to take the depression offered to us.

Who Convinced You?

Let me ask you this: who took the time, and when did they take the time to convince you that you cannot become a millionaire? If not, how did you become convinced of it?

Let's think again of that person we mentioned earlier. Let's say that years ago they received a word that they would go to the nations. Did those nations just suddenly appear? Will the person easily and automatically go to every one of those nations? No. They must persevere in that word, believing God for every step of it to be fulfilled, and doing their part to make it happen. Just because you receive a word does not mean that it will automatically and easily be fulfilled. You have to start sowing seed actions toward that goal God has set before you.

When you first hear a word that God wants to do something in and through you, then you must become that word. And when you become that word, nothing can prevent you from fulfilling all that God has spoken to you.

How To Change Your Life

Can you now see how to change your life and how to change your ministry and stop the devil from knocking at your door? Hear the Word, believe the Word, and become the Word.

God said:

Out of the mouth of babes and sucklings hast thou ordained strength because of thine enemies, that thou mightest still the enemy and the avenger. Psalm 8:2

There is strength in the seed that we cannot yet comprehend. Everything about the seed's future is in that seed. All you are to become is already in you. There is nothing missing. So when the devil comes and says to you, "Let's prove a point," let him know in no uncertain terms that there is no point to be proven. There is nothing else that we are supposed to become.

Understanding the Seed, Part I

We are already it. The full potential is in the seed, and we are the seed. Thank God!

Nothing Is Lacking

To help us understand this truth, God has seen to it that each woman alive has the potential within her to produce children after her kind. All of that potential is there within her. Nothing is lacking. She does not need to become like some other woman to have children of her own. She is her own woman.

In the same way, what each of us needs in our churches is not to be found in some other church. Oh, yes, others may have beautiful choirs and talented people, but God has placed within *your* church the potential it requires to fulfill its destiny. Nothing is lacking.

The same is true personally. Everything that you need to become the fullness of God's plan for your life already resides within you.

When Jesus called Peter (and Andrew), He said to him: *"Follow me, and I will make you fishers of men"* (Matthew 4:19). What was Peter in that moment? He was already a fisherman. Why didn't Jesus use some different word to describe what Peter would become? Because Peter was already a fisherman. He would now just become a better fisherman and a fisher of men.

Before Jesus had met Nathaniel personally, He already knew him and said of him:

Understanding the Seed

Behold an Israelite indeed, in whom is no guile!
John 1:47

He was calling the people He met by what they already were.

Why didn't He go to Thomas and say, "Son, behold your mother?" Thomas would not have responded to that, as John did. God will not come to you and tell you something that is farfetched. The truth about it is this: every prophetic word you receive is reasoned. The full potential of it is all already in you. It will not come when you move to some other great ministry, and everything will suddenly fall into place, and you will become the minister you are destined to become. It will happen by you staying exactly where God has placed you.

STOP WANTING TO BE LIKE OTHER PEOPLE

Stop wanting to be like other people. If your eyes could be opened to see into other people's prayer times, you would be amazed. Some pray, "Oh, God, give me Paul Yongi Cho's kind of church." But do you think you have the stamina to handle a ministry like that? If you are not made for that, the pressures of it would break you. So let the seed "seed" itself and produce its own unique fruit.

I know that when you quote this to someone else, they will say, "What kind of language is that?" But who cares, as long as people are understanding this powerful truth. After that we can talk about sowing, using the nicer grammatical phrases.

Understanding the Seed, Part I

This is what religion has done to us. It has crippled us in many areas. "Do X number of things, X number of times, and do it like this, and you will be okay." Who even wants that kind of religion? Do you really want that? Not me.

Giving Is Sowing

The Scriptures tell us:

Give, and it shall be given to you; good measure, pressed down, and shaken together, and running over, shall men give into your bosom.   Luke 6:38

This word *give* is another word for sowing. Or, let's go back to the language we have been using — "seeding":

Seed, and you shall receive seed; good measure, pressed down, and shaken together, and running over, shall men seed unto your bosom.

Seeds Produce After Their Kind

Let me show you another truth about the seed:

Genesis 1:20-21
[20] *And God said, Let the waters bring forth abundantly the moving creature that hath life, and fowl that may fly above the earth in the open firmament of heaven.*
[21] *And God created great whales, and every living creature that moveth, which the waters brought forth abundantly,*

after their kind, and every winged fowl after his kind: and God saw that it was good.

The Bible is saying that God spoke to the waters and said, "Produce your kind." That "kind" was fish and whales, and all such things. That's what water normally produces, but here water also produced birds.

God produces whales by speaking to the seed that has that ability, but if you were to find a whale near your home, where there is no sea or even a pond, what would you be thinking? *"No! I did not see that."* Right? Because there is no way a whale could be there. Whales are not supposed to be on land. Seeds produce after their kind.

God spoke to the earth that was to create a harvest:

And God said, Let the earth bring forth grass, the herb yielding seed, and the fruit tree yielding fruit after his kind, whose seed is in itself, upon the earth: and it was so. Genesis 1:11

If you found grass growing on a human being, what would you think? *"Something is wrong here."* Why? Because the earth brings forth grass, and human beings don't. Seeds produce after their kind.

SEEDTIME AND HARVEST

From the very beginning, God established seedtime and harvest time. This was not a strange concept that came about later on. God established it early on. "If you want this fruit," He was declaring, "here's what you should do — always."

Now here is the interesting part. This is something the devil needs to hear from you. I am sure that he talks to you, and that's why I am emphasizing this:

Genesis 1:20, 24, and 26
> *20 And God said, Let the waters bring forth abundantly the moving creature that hath life, and fowl that may fly above the earth in the open firmament of heaven.*
> *24 And God said, Let the earth bring forth the living creature after his kind, cattle, and creeping thing, and beast of the earth after his kind: and it was so.*
> *26 And God said, Let us make man in our image, after our likeness: and let them have dominion over the fish of the sea, and over the fowl of the air, and over the cattle, and over all the earth, and over every creeping thing that creepeth upon the earth.*

You are the product of the living God, and that is the reason you are to have dominion. The Bible says, *"Let them have dominion."* You were born to exercise dominion. Yes, man lost that right in the Fall, but because Jesus died, His redemption brought us back to our rightful place. You are a being created for dominance. What could be more wonderful?

DOMINATE THE STORM

Because we know the promises of God, the days just ahead will be very interesting. This will be a time of great floods, meaning there will be a lot of drama in many ministries. Many ministries (and individual children of God) will be hit by violent storms. But, no matter how much the storm tossed the boat Jesus was in, He could sleep and sleep well. He had a very soft pillow, and He was not afraid of a storm. He knew that He was its master.

This is the dominance which you and I have been called to walk in. We are life's masters, and we can sleep on a soft pillow, even as storms rage all around us. We have been called to a place of total rest in Jesus.

It really does not matter what the coming floods will be like. You will keep building your ministry in the midst of them. You will keep doing what God has called you to do. You will establish His will upon the floods.

You and I are more than equal to the task at hand. We are *"seated far above"* (Ephesians 1:21). That's how far above we are, above whatever the devil is planning to do next.

Change Will Come from Today

From today, your ministry will change. You can now experience more manifestation of God's promises to you. Because your thoughts are changing, so are your ways. And that means you will soon reap a great harvest.

You have new dominion. The next time a headache touches your child, just say, "I have been created by God Himself," and the devil will have to flee. He is in trouble when you discover who you are.

You are a product of the most high God, and redemption has perfected your gift. So, when Jesus said, *"And these signs shall follow them that believe; ... they shall lay hands on the sick, and they shall recover"* (Mark 16:18), He was saying, "In My name, this is what you should be doing. In My place, this is what you should be doing. Just do what I would do in the same situation. When you do what I would do, you will receive a harvest."

God Is Getting Himself Some Honor

Our God is getting Himself victory through the insignificant, small, base and foolish things, and in the process, He is confounding the wisdom of this world (see 1 Corinthians 1:27). And He is having fun doing it. He said to Moses:

> *I will get me honour upon Pharaoh, and upon all his host, upon his chariots, and upon his horsemen. And the Egyptians shall know that I am the L*ORD*, when I have gotten me honour upon Pharaoh, upon his chariots, and upon his horsemen.* Exodus 14:17-18

And God is saying to you:

"From your boss, who has been giving you trouble, I will get Me glory. From that witchcraft that has been spoken over your family, I will get Me some glory. If you will just know who you are and stick to it, I will get Me some glory. You do not need to run back to Egypt. That is no longer your home."

Understanding the Seed

The Potential Is in You

Jesus said:

For there is nothing hid, which shall not be manifested; neither was any thing kept secret, but that it should come abroad.   Mark 4:22

You cannot hide the potential of a seed. It is within, and your potential in within you. Yes, you are a demon-chasing, mountain-moving, dead-raising Christian. You have all of that inside of you. Don't worry about going somewhere else to get it. You have it. It is already there within you.

Take Heed What You Hear

Jesus continued:

And he said unto them, Take heed what ye hear: with what measure ye mete, it shall be measured to you: and unto you that hear shall more be given.   Mark 4:24

What you hear does not stop on the outside of you; it goes on in, and it can have an impact — for good or for evil. The Word of God is saying here, "If someone with authority were to go to a seed and say to it, 'Become a bean seed,' it would eventually become a bean seed." This means you have to be careful what you are listening to. The more of the Word of God you listen to, the more you will become what that Word says.

Understanding the Seed, Part I

When you get a phone call and someone asks you, "Is it okay if I come around? We'll just hang out." You need to ask, "Hang out to do what? To talk about what?" When you are determined to walk in the Spirit, your ears will become attentive to what others are saying, and if it's not right, something inside of you will tell you to stay away from that person.

Don't Even Joke with Them

Don't even joke with them. Too often, what we joke about comes to pass. Kidding words produce a harvest.

I heard a chilling story of what happened to a very powerful man of faith through joking. God was using him, even to raise the dead in Africa. One day he was sitting around the table with some friends, and he began to joke with one of them, "If you drink from this glass, you will immediately go to Heaven."

The man said, "No, thank you."

The man of God brought the glass back to himself, and they continued their conversation. Awhile later, forgetting what he had said, he drank from the glass himself, and that day He died and went to Heaven. You really have to be very careful with your words. They are more powerful than you know.

Some Christians have severe standards of conduct and others feel that we just need to have fun out of life. I'm kind of in the middle. I agree that Christians should have fun, but I must insist that we be careful about the type of people we are having our fun with and the type of fun we are getting into.

Can Christians go to movies? Go, but be careful about what you watch and listen to, and be careful of the ideas you take home with you. For instance, many women come away from a movie thinking that their husband should look and act like Denzel Washington. If you are one of those who think Denzel is the thing, be careful. As a minister of the Gospel, we have standards to uphold. We can't start acting and talking like someone else.

Some women in the church want their husbands to be just like their pastor, and some men want their wives to be like a certain sister who can sing well. But God knows what He is doing. Stop trying to be like someone else. The things God has in store for you are so great that there isn't time to be fooling around. Stop being men-pleasers and start being God-pleasers.

You have a future, and you are getting there step by step. God has a plan for your life in the days ahead, so stop saying, "What will be will be." You will have to show me a scripture to support that. I have not found one yet.

Vision vs. Planning

As we were growing up, our family was very big on vision. *"Where there is no vision, the people perish"* (Proverbs 29:18). People become stale bread, water that is just standing, almost like a Dead Sea. So, to us, vision was everything. In time, however, I discovered that you can have a vision and not know how to carry that vision out. It doesn't just happen. We have to work at it.

We could say, "Without a plan, a vision is pointless." We need to have a plan, and we need to work that plan out.

Being in ministry is not enough. What is the plan? What do you hope to accomplish in the days ahead?

Far too many of us make New Year's resolutions and never get beyond that. I like how someone said it: "I have graduated from resolutions. I now put down a plan."

Our resolutions, all too often, are spoken out of emotion. At the end of each year, we should be able to seek the face of the Lord, hear what He is saying about the year to come, and then work with Him toward bringing His will to pass.

I am not moved by the titles of those who are considered to be great Christian leaders of our day, and you must not be either. Listen to God. Ask Him, "Is this where You want me to be? If I am here, will I be the seed that I am supposed to be?" He overcomes with seeds. What kind of seed are you?

What Type of Vessel Are You?

God says in His Word:

But in a great house there are not only vessels of gold and of silver, but also of wood and of earth; and some to honour, and some to dishonour. 2 Timothy 2:20

What type of vessel are you? God has spoken into your life. Will you allow Him to continue speaking? It is only as He is speaking into you that you have that seed in you.

His Word declares:

Whosoever is born of God doth not commit sin; for his seed remaineth in him: and he cannot sin, because he is born of God. 1 John 3:9

If you have ever sought the face of God, this is the time. If you have ever held the horns of the altar, this is the time.

Lord,

Begin the work in us, and thank You, Father, for doing it.

Amen!

Chapter 4

Recognizing the Lord of the Harvest
by Dr. Harold McDougal

God has an amazing family all over the earth, and I'm glad to be part of it. Anywhere we go, we can find tongue-talking, shouting people who love the Lord. Thank God for His people among the nations.

Our Final Victory

The Bible lesson that begins with 1 Corinthians 15:50 in my New King James Version of the Bible is entitled *Our Final Victory*. That sounds good to me. It says this:

> Now this I say, brethren, that flesh and blood cannot inherit the kingdom of God; nor does corruption inherit incorruption. [51] Behold, I tell you a mystery: We shall not all sleep, but we shall all be changed— [52] in a moment, in the twinkling of an eye, at the last trumpet. For the trumpet will sound, and the dead will be raised incor-

ruptible, and we shall be changed. ⁵³ For this corruptible must put on incorruption, and this mortal must put on immortality. ⁵⁴ So when this corruptible has put on incorruption, and this mortal has put on immortality, then shall be brought to pass the saying that is written: "Death is swallowed up in victory."
⁵⁵ "O Death, where is your sting? O Hades, where is your victory?" ⁵⁶ The sting of death is sin, and the strength of sin is the law. ⁵⁷ But thanks be to God, who gives us the victory through our Lord Jesus Christ.
58 Therefore, my beloved brethren, be steadfast, immovable, always abounding in the work of the Lord, knowing that your labor is not in vain in the Lord.

                    1 Corinthians 15:50-58, NKJV

"The trumpet WILL sound," so get ready. "The dead WILL be raised incorruptible." They're ready. And what else? "We SHALL be changed." Oh, I like that. This passage ends with those wonderful words: "But thanks be to God who gives us the victory through our Lord Jesus Christ." Are you thankful today?

This chapter of First Corinthians could end right there, and we would be blessed. Just to know that a final victory is coming, and that all pain will cease is something wonderful to contemplate. No more sickness, no more tears, no more sorrow, no more suffering. All of that will be cast aside, and we will put on something so very wonderful that I'm sure we cannot yet begin to comprehend it. Eternity will be far beyond anything we have imagined it to be.

Taken To Heaven

In Louisiana, we attend a wonderful church in Hammond pastored by Lloyd and Regina Blount. One of the speakers who comes there sometimes lives in Norway. She died and was taken into Heaven several times during a serious bout of Crohn's disease. Doctors declared her dead, and before she came back, she was able to spend time in Heaven. What she described was breathtaking, and we urgently need to get her testimonies into print.

Heaven is so wonderful that it is currently beyond our comprehension, beyond our ability to understand. Just know that it will be so wonderful that you will be totally happy there in the presence of God. Don't miss it for any reason. Don't get bypassed in our final victory.

Don't Argue Over the Timing

Long ago I stopped arguing about the timing of our going or exactly how it will happen. We've argued about those things far too long. The truth is that only the Lord knows the details for sure. What we must be concerned about is being ready ourselves and helping others to get ready.

When sickness comes your way, or you experience pain and sorrow (and these come to all of us), think of this passage, meditate on our final victory, and know that all that is contrary to that final victory will one day be overcome. There will be no tears in Heaven. None! And what we are experiencing in God's presence in these days is just a foretaste of the Glory to come.

Understanding the Seed

We Must Do Something

The passage could have ended there, and it would have been a wonderful message to the Church, but it did not end there. There is another important element to all of this. It is found in verse 58 and begins with the word *"therefore."* This refers back to what was being said in the preceding verses. In other words, because we are planning for a final victory and we know our end, we must do something. Because we have these great promises from God, because His power is over all other power, because of who He is and who we are in Him, because in the end we win and will rule and reign with Jesus, we must do something.

And What Is that Something?

What is that something?

Therefore, my beloved brethren, be steadfast, immovable, always abounding in the work of the Lord, knowing that your labor is not in vain in the Lord.

What are we to always abound in? The work of the Lord. What are we to know? That our labor is not in vain in the Lord.

Are you steadfast and immovable? This means that we must not slip back tomorrow, next week, or next month. We must hold the ground we have won. We must stand strong against every enemy. It means that we must keep pressing forward. There is no retreat in our God.

There are many wonderful truths here, but I want to concentrate on the *work* part, the *labor* that is *not in vain*.

Discovering Calvary Campground

I attended my first campmeeting at Calvary Campground in Ashland, Virginia, in 1965. I had met Ruth Ward Heflin in India in January of 1964, and after I had gotten back from a wonderful year-long seventeen-nation ministry adventure late that year, I went to Ashland to meet the rest of the family. They lived in a humble three-bedroom block house on a dirt road (now beautifully paved and named Heflin Lane in their honor). The house was built before anything existed on the campground and before the land that eventually made up the camp had been donated. Before that, everything that now makes up Calvary Campground was nothing more than a seed in their spirits.

My life was never the same from the moment I met the Heflins. When you met a Heflin, you were forever changed. Your life was turned upside down because they were such wonderful people.

For one thing, the Heflins, all of them, never stopped telling wonderful stories about the goodness of the Lord. That was their passion. That was the air they breathed. Any moment of any day was a good time to learn something new and exciting about the Lord.

I don't remember how many days I spent with the Heflins that first time, but it was long enough to see what they were like, and there were many things I loved about them, enough to know that I wanted to be around them more in the future. So I went back that next summer for the campmeeting, and I stayed for many weeks afterward to help them build cabins to accommodate more people.

THE CAMP WORK ETHIC

One of the most remarkable attributes of the Heflin family was that they were some of the hardest working people I had ever met. They slept only a few hours each night (partly because they received phone calls at all hours from people needing their prayers).

After camp was over, and the building had begun, late every afternoon we would quickly shower and dress and then drive at least an hour to another town (I think it was West Point, Virginia, that time) where they had one of their tents set up, and we would conduct a crusade. One week of that meeting, they had me preach. I was young and could work all day and then go to church at night, but that was just the beginning.

We stayed every night until every single person had been prayed for, and then they would talk to anyone who would listen, and before we could get started back home, it was past midnight. Back at home, they would sit around the table and tell more stories about miracles they had seen in days gone by. That meant we didn't get to bed until after two o'clock. Still, early the next morning (in fact, at 6:00 A.M.) Father Heflin was knocking on our bedroom door shouting, "Time to get up! There's lots of work to be done down at the campground. We have to get some serious work done for God today. So, rise and shine!" And he wasn't satisfied with just knocking and calling out. Next, he opened the door and came in to make sure we had gotten the message and were getting up. Anybody who stayed in his house worked for God.

"Rise and shine?" Already? I felt like we had just gotten to bed. But no one could say no to Wallace Heflin. He had a way of bringing you around to his way of thinking ... and quickly. He was a no-nonsense kind of guy.

What We Remember about Wallace Heflin, Sr.

When we think of Wallace Heflin, Sr., we are reminded of his great vision. He did many crusades at great personal cost and in the process raised up many churches. At the same time, he raised up many great men and women of faith. He also preached in many nations and saw great miracles of healing in his ministry.

Still, when I think of the man, I see him praying and then marking off the corners of buildings that should be built for God's glory. He would pace the distance out as he was being led by the Spirit. In this way, he laid out the dimensions for most of the major buildings.

I also see him on the tractor, pulling down trees so that more roads and buildings could be built on the property. All of the Heflins loved trees, and they tried to save every tree they could so that the area could remain covered as much as possible, it could be used as a shelter in difficult times. But some trees had to come down, and he was just the man for the job. From the time the man got his first cup of coffee in the morning, he was off, doing whatever he saw needed done in God's Kingdom and involving as many people as possible in the process.

It was a very common sight to see him walking to wherever he was going, with his arm around some younger man, telling him stories of what happened when he went to Jamaica, what God did for him and the family in India, and how God had moved in Haiti. He never tired of telling it. He was never too tired to encourage someone coming up in ministry and never too tired to do some more work for God. He loved the passage that declares: *"As thy days, so shall thy strength be,"* (Deuteronomy 33:25), and he took it literally.

What We Remember about Mother Heflin

When we think of Mother Heflin, his wife (Edith Ward Heflin), the first thing that comes to mind is that she and her husband were the founders of that great ministry. We remember her teaching every day during camptime in the eleven o'clock service. She also loved to teach the children and would never miss an opportunity to do it. She felt like she was raising up future servants of God, and she instilled in them the faith that had kept her and her family for so many years. She challenged them to do great things for God.

But let me tell you a few things about her that most do not know. When the camp program was started, there were no sleeping facilities or eating facilities. Everyone who came to stay slept in the three-bedroom Heflin house, and everyone ate there too. She cooked for them and served them herself. When other people came just for the day, there was no space to get them in the house, so she had folding chairs arranged around the back door, and she served their meals out that door.

There was never enough food for everyone, but she was accustomed to that and knew what to do. She took what she had and began to pray over it, believing God that it would somehow feed everyone who needed to be fed. If you haven't read her book, *I Serve a God of Miracles,* [1] you need to. There are many more wonderful stories there.

When gasoline was in short supply during the Great Depression, and she and Dad Heflin needed to get to their next preaching place, they had to pray over the gasoline and believe God to multiply it. This happened so many times for them that it became something of a family tradition, and their son and daughter did the same thing. When I would ride long distances with Brother Heflin, Jr., he would make me very nervous. I would look over at the fuel gauge, and the needle was below zero. I would say, "Brother, I think we need to pull over and get some gas."

"Have faith in God, my brother," he would say. "We don't have time to stop. We'll get there." And we always did.

Once the first cabins were built, as people arrived for campmeeting, Mother Heflin personally escorted them to their cabin. (I know this because she did it for me, and I saw her doing it for others.) She asked them to wait

---
1. Shippensburg, PA, Destiny Image Publishers: 1991

outside for a few minutes, and she went inside, swept the cabin, and made the bed for them. Before leaving, she asked if there was anything else they needed. If there was, she sent someone to get it for them. She showed each visitor where all of the important buildings were on the grounds (there were not nearly as many at the time). Then she went to the kitchen to start cooking for them. That's what the Heflins were like.

What We Remember about Ruth Ward Heflin

When we think of Ruth Ward Heflin, who for many years was my dearest friend in the world, what do we think of? We think of her going to most every nation on earth to carry the Gospel. We think of how she broke down the barriers to women ministers in many countries. She was instrumental in opening entire countries that had previously been closed to the Gospel.

We think of what she did in Israel. Not only did she establish and maintain a place where worship could ascend on high from Mount Zion; she welcomed people from all nations to that place and fed and housed them while they were in the land. She organized and sent out teams to many nations of the world, calling the Jews back to the land and helping them to get there.

Ruth was a regular campmeeting speaker for many years. She usually preached the first two weeks of summer campmeeting. Then, after the passing of her brother, she came back to America and headed up the entire ministry for several years. Her books have been read by millions in many languages, and her many songs have been and continue to be sung around the world.

At her funeral, representatives from many of the largest ministries in the world came to pay their respects, and the heartfelt eulogies they offered filled many evenings. So many great people were on the platform the day of the funeral that we could not give them all time. Ruth Ward Heflin was a great lady.

Now, with all of that in mind, would you believe that Ruth and her father built with their own hands the first cabins on the campgrounds? It's true. She was just a teenager at the time, and her brother was still out wandering in sin, so she became her father's helper, and they did the building. Above all else, a Heflin was a worker for God.

At Calvary Campground, Everyone Works

When people began coming to Calvary Campground to live, wanting to be in that wonderful prayerful and faith-filled atmosphere, they were always expected to work. Prayer is wonderful and all of us need more of it. Worship is wonderful and we all need to do it more. But there is a lot of WORK that needs to be done in the Kingdom of God. The problem, as I see it, is that most of us today attempt to define the work we are willing to do and, in doing so, we also define the work we are not willing to do:

"This, but not that."

"My calling is to _____, not _____."
"I wasn't called to wash dishes."
"I wasn't called to move dirt."
"I wasn't called to rake leaves."

What does the Bible have to say about all of this? It says:

Whatever your hand finds to do, do it with your might.
Ecclesiastes 9:10

What are we to do with our might? Whatever! And what does that mean? It means whatever needs to be done. Whatever is in front of us.

This dedication to a work ethic for love of God is one of the reasons I have loved this family so much, and this work ethic became the foundation for the campground and its ministries throughout the world. That was how it started, and that was how it has moved forward ever since.

"But how could people work so hard and sleep so little and still remain alive?" people have often asked me. Those who lived here had to learn a secret. There was supernatural strength to be had in God.

As I noted before, Wallace Heflin, Sr., the founder of the work, loved the biblical passage that says: *"As your days, so shall your strength be"* (Deuteronomy 33:25). He took that literally, and he practiced it religiously. He believed that whatever his day (and night) held, God would give him the corresponding strength. And it worked for him. For sure the Heflins could not have had normal strength. With all the long hours they were putting in, praying, going to church every night of the week, ministering to the sick wherever they were to be found, and then sleeping very few hours night after night, that would have been impossible. They lived on that supernatural strength.

WHAT WE REMEMBER ABOUT WALLACE HEFLIN, JR.

When we think about Wallace Heflin, Jr., what do we remember? Personally I loved going to the nations with him, and hundreds of people traveled with him over the years and gained wonderful experience in ministry among the nations. Every year, he traveled twice to Israel for meetings, and he did meetings in other countries along the way going there and also on the way back home. This included Egypt, Jordan, Syria, Lebanon, Greece, Italy, Turkey, and many others. When China opened, he began taking groups twice a year to minister there. The same was true with Russia. He did crusades all across the former Soviet Union.

He sent me ahead of him twice to Russia. On one of those occasions, he would be coming later with a team of forty ministers, and I was to work with the local pastors to prepare the locations, get the advertising ready, and anything else that was needed. Just before I left, he handed me a huge sum of cash that I then would have to distribute as needed. On the flights over, I had money hidden all over me. It was a rather frightening experience. And that was just one year. He did that every year for many years.

One of the most difficult things about all of that travel was the constant time changes. This was particularly hard on him since he slept so little anyway. He seemed to always be in some other time zone. For most people, this was exhausting, and I never fully understood how he did it. No wonder the man fell asleep when he sat too long in any one place! His life was so full of activity for God.

This is not to mention the many campmeetings, conferences, tent crusades, and church revivals he preached. If he ever found himself with a few minutes of spare time, he felt like a sinner and asked God to forgive him for his backsliding.

THE HEALING MINISTRY

Wallace Heflin, Jr. was a powerful preacher, and we have his books as a legacy of that gift. But he also had a great healing ministry. He prayed for people all over the world, and God did great miracles. As he entered any crusade or special meeting, he had his eye out for sick people, especially those who had visible defects, could not walk properly, or were on crutches or in a wheelchair. At some point in the service, he would call them to the front before everyone and believe for the miracle they needed. To him, nothing was too hard for the Lord, and he made sure God got all the glory for the healings that resulted.

I cannot forget the night we were on live television in the Philippines in an open-air crusade in the capital city. Our airtime had about run out when he began to pray for a woman with a large goiter on her neck. As he prayed, that goiter deflated and disappeared and all that was left was loose skin where it had been. The owner of the television station had been watching, and now he called to his technicians who were operating the equipment in the truck and said, "Tell those preachers that if they can produce some more miracles like that one I'll give them the next hour of airtime free of charge." God didn't fail us, and every night of that crusade was televised.

Later, I was able to have a weekly program on that same television channel. It was live for one full hour, and we did it from the church. Whatever God was doing or whatever He was saying, that's what went out over the airwaves, and it brought great revival.

How God Did It

Interestingly enough, during that great crusade in Quezon City, the actual crusade crowd was much smaller than anticipated. The reason was that there was a transportation strike. We were praying for this to end quickly, since our thought was to have as large a crowd as possible at the crusade sight. As it turned out, the strike was the best thing that could have happened. People had to stay home, and they were watching as God did those great miracles. This sparked a great revival. Our audience was estimated to be many times more than we could have expected to have at the actual crusade.

Before long, we began to get telephone calls from people saying, "We saw those wonderful miracles. Could you teach us to pray like that?" Perhaps most importantly, some of those calls were from nuns and priests. The first nuns who called were cloistered. They had dedicated their lives to prayer, and yet they had never seen anything like this. "Could you come and teach us?" they asked, and we did. The rest is history. Two years later, *Time* magazine reported that one thousand priests and nuns and ten thousand Catholic laypeople in the Philippines had been baptized in the Spirit and were now speaking in tongues.

WHAT ELSE DID HE DO?

All of that began with the healing ministry of Wallace Heflin Jr. It would take many books to tell all that he accomplished in his lifetime for God, but would you believe that he personally welded the steel beams that support many of the larger camp buildings? They were used and rather rough when he was able to buy them. He had to use a wire brush to clean them up, and then, since there was no one on the campground who knew how to weld, he taught himself and did all the welding himself. This is all the more phenomenal when you realize that he had been a salesman in his early years and had never done physical labor.

Wallace Heflin has been gone for many years now, but as the Scriptures declare, his *"works do follow"* him (Revelation 14:13). Great meetings can be held in comfort today because he was dedicated to working for God.

WORK! WORK! WORK!

For many years, when God spoke to him in prophecy, He would say, "Work, work, work, work, work." Brother

Heflin once complained to his mother about this. Was "work" the only thing God had to say to him? What about his great call? "Son," she would tell him, "we can't control the Holy Ghost. If He says, 'work,' then work it is." And so he kept working.

That first summer I spent at the camp, I couldn't help but notice how much he loved his beautiful red Pontiac, and yet there he was hauling mattresses from building to building on the hood of that fine car. Even the car was now dedicated to work for God. Wallace Heflin did anything and everything that needed to be done. Nothing was beneath him. Nothing! These were people who were ready to work for God. What work? Whatever it took to get the job done.

Released

Eventually the day came that God released him from all the physical work. Others had come in, and they could now help with the various responsibilities. He was relieved. But now his duties shifted to administration, and it was always difficult to see how he could keep up with it all.

I was in Russia another time on his behalf, and I felt that I needed to call him because the coup had taken place that toppled Mikhail Gorbachev from power. The Russian people were terrified, not knowing what to expect next. The atmosphere had suddenly turned so bad that local believers said to me, "Brother, you need to cancel those crusades. It's too dangerous. I'm sure your friend will not want to come under these conditions."

I hated to call him because it was nighttime in Ashland, during the few hours he usually slept, but I had no choice. "I am so sorry to call you at this time of the night," I began. "I know you need your sleep, but I needed to consult with you on an important issue."

He was not upset at all about having been awakened from sleep. If someone needed him, they could wake him up at any hour. "What is it?" he asked.

I quickly explained the situation to him, ending with the words, "The local believers are rather nervous about your safety and suggest that you might want to postpone the trip until another time."

He said, "You tell them we will be there on the date we said we would be there, and God will take care of us. We're going to have a great crusade." Nothing moved a Heflin when there was work to be done for God.

What about You and Me?

What about you and me? Nothing should be beneath us when it comes to God's work. The Scriptures are so very clear on this point. They say that those who use the talents they have been given will receive more. Jesus' words to them are :

> *Well done, thou good and faithful servant: thou hast been faithful over a few things, I will make thee ruler over many things: enter thou into the joy of thy lord.*
>
> Matthew 25:21

However, those who refuse to use what they have been given will be severely judged:

> *Thou wicked and slothful servant, thou knewest that I reap where I sowed not, and gather where I have not strawed: 27 Thou oughtest therefore to have put my money to the exchangers, and then at my coming I should have received mine own with usury.*
> *28 Take therefore the talent from him, and give it unto him which hath ten talents.*
> *29 For unto every one that hath shall be given, and he shall have abundance: but from him that hath not shall be taken away even that which he hath.*
> *30 And cast ye the unprofitable servant into outer darkness: there shall be weeping and gnashing of teeth.*
> Matthew 25:26-30

Strangely this man seems to have appreciated his talent and its value, so he hid it in the ground. When he later approached his lord, he was very proud of himself, thinking that he had done a good and wise thing. He must have been surprised when judgment was pronounced upon him and his one talent was taken from him and given to those who were willing to use their talents for the lord.

What does all of this mean to us on a practical level? The same people will be called on to do many different things because they have proven themselves to be faithful and trustworthy. That's not a punishment; it's a reward. The Lord's command is to take from those who have not been using their talents and give to those who are using theirs. And that is key to the Kingdom of God.

When you are doing faithfully what you already know to do, then the Lord will show you another step. If you haven't even taken the first step, how can He show you another one? How can He give you a greater vision when you haven't fulfilled your first responsibility?

First God shows us simple things to do. Sometimes they seem humiliating. Humiliation is related to the word humble, so it's not always a bad thing. We could all use more humility. As we decrease, He increases, and our lives become more fruitful.

The Scriptures are so clear. When we have been faithful over a few things, then God makes us ruler over many things. When does this happen? When we have been faithful over the first few things — whatever they happen to be.

These "few things" may not seem to be so important. Some say, "But this is not my vision. I saw myself preaching on a great platform in Africa." That's fine, and that vision will come true one day … IF you are faithful in the few things you are given to do today. If you are faithful in the lesser things, then the Lord will raise you up to do the greater things.

Ministry Is Work

The ministry is work. It's not a throne that you sit on, ruling over your little kingdom and calling for your subjects to bring you the things you need. We've seen that too many times. And what happens when we begin to exalt ourselves? We are humbled, are we not?

This is an automatic process. It's guaranteed, and it never fails:

> *For whoever exalts himself will be humbled, and he who humbles himself will be exalted.*   Luke 14:11, NKJV

Those are the words of Jesus, and He was very serious. There's no need to ask if the humbling will really come. It will come all right. You can count on it. It's automatic. *Whoever* includes you, and it includes me. Who will be humbled? *Whoever* exalts himself. Who will be exalted? *Whoever* humbles himself. *Whoever*! It's a spiritual law that can never be broken.

Pride is an enormous temptation.

> *I'm an apostle now.*
> *I've been officially commissioned by the church.*
> *I have been ordained.*
> *I carry an official missionary license.*

If saying something like this comes from pride, it is the beginning of that person's downfall, and they will definitely not do great things for God.

WHAT WE THINK ABOUT JANE JOWDER

When we think about Sarah Jane Lowder, the current director of Calvary Campground, what do we think of?

She has an important position these days, as director of that beautiful facility. She is the one to welcome us all and provide for us all. She has lots of help doing it, and she has to believe the Lord to make it possible, but she is the one who actually does it. She brings in the wonderful speakers who bless us all. She makes sure everything is running smoothly so that we can all concentrate on getting God's blessing.

But I remember a time when I would see her driving around a crazy-looking trash truck the camp had. She would go from building to building gathering up all the trash to take it to the dump. I remember seeing her outside of the dining hall unloading a truck full of great sacks of food and carrying them into a storeroom. Some remember the day she was down inside the excavation for the camp dining hall, cleaning out the mud so that the basement could be built. Most camp visitors these days have never seen her do things like that, so they wouldn't remember her in that way. That's the type of person she is.

For more than twenty years, Sister Jane Lowder served in the camp kitchen and dish room. She washed pots and pans, mopped the floors, and did whatever else needed to be done. For years, she was the official woodcutter and wood splitter for the camp. She knew how to do it, so she was elected for the job.

STRUGGLING TO FIND A PLACE?

There are many things to be done in the church today, and yet God's people are struggling to find what they should be doing. One of our problems is that we are so rich now that we prefer to hire a professional janitor than to allow God's people to develop their talents. We pay professional painters to spruce everything up periodically. When we need something built, we hire professionals to build it. And then we wonder why there is no anointing and no glory flowing in our midst. We all need to be working for God. What should we be doing? Whatever our hands find to do.

The Summer of 1965

That first summer, after campmeeting had ended (in those days it was only a month long), I decided that I wanted to stay on. There was no heat anywhere on the camp, and the buildings were now closed up until the next season. So we stayed with the Heflins in their house again. Wallace Jr. and Ruth had grown accustomed, since childhood, to giving up their rooms and their beds for others to sleep in. To tell you the truth, I don't know where they were sleeping at the time. On the floor somewhere no doubt. They never mentioned it. That's the kind of people they were.

By staying in their home with them, it became clear to us that this lifestyle was not just a one-week thing or a one-month thing. This was their lifestyle, every day and all year long. This was what they did.

Dad Heflin was not happy if he was not in church somewhere every single night. If he was not preaching somewhere, then he wanted to go support someone who was. He would find somewhere to go and get as many others as possible to go with him. It was not uncommon for the Heflin vehicles (just cars in those days) to carry four full-sized adults in front and at least that many and sometimes more in back. Once you got packed in you could barely move, but everyone was happy and blessed. It might take an hour or more to get to the meeting place, but when you got there, everyone jumped out praising God and ready to set the world on fire. And this went on night after night.

How Many Can Do This?

Now let me ask you this: How many churches that you know of have a campground where they invite everyone to come and be blessed and don't charge anything for the privilege? Personally I don't know of any, as rich as our American churches are today. CPT has never been rich. It has never had millionaires in its congregation. It has never been made up of the affluent. God has done this for them because of their dedication to His work and their willingness to do whatever it takes to get the job done.

Mother Heflin's Ministry of Prophecy and Bottle Caps

Mother Heflin had such a sweet and powerful ministry of prophecy that people came here from all over the world just to have her lay hands on them and pray. They knew they would never be the same again. I knew missionaries who would periodically fly in here from New York just to get a word from her.

But there was something amazing that Edith Heflin would do with her spare time, aside from taking care of her grandchildren (which was a job in itself). The camp had a small snack bar that sold soft drinks, and the cola bottles had a top that could be flipped off. As people carried their drinks around the campground, those tops would get dropped and scattered all over the place (along with chewing gum wrappers and other litter). Any time Mother Heflin had some spare time, she would go around with a little pail gathering up all of that litter and trying to make the campground a more appealing place for everyone. She loved the place. To her it was God's place, a place to be appreciated and taken care of.

We need more Edith Heflins in our world today. I'm not saying that you have to be the trash person the rest of your life. What I'm saying is: start doing what you know needs to be done, and God will lift you higher.

Learn from the Carpenter of Galilee

In my time, I have done plenty of carpentry work for the Kingdom. I knew nothing about carpentry, but the wonderful thing is that Jesus was a carpenter. I talked to Him, and He helped me. I had the privilege of helping to build churches in many places. I didn't think for a minute that because I was the director, such work was beneath me or doing it somehow demeaned me. Not at all! I had other things that I could have been dedicating my time to, but that work needed to be done, so I did it.

At a certain point, I had to learn how to lay concrete blocks. I hadn't known how before. I watched others doing it, prayed, and then started doing it too. Let me tell you a wonderful little story about laying blocks on the campground.

Laying Blocks on the Campground

Wallace Jr. and I laid the blocks for the entire row of buildings on the lower camp road. One day, when we were building one of those cabins, he was trying to insert one of the used window frames into the blocks we had already laid. The opening was a little tight, and so he took a hammer and began taping on the frame. Suddenly it broke free and fell into place, but in the process he injured his hand. Some small jagged pieces of glass had been left in that frame, and when it fell into place, one of those triangular pieces of glass plunged into the top of his hand. It hit something, because blood began spurting out.

He turned to me and asked me to pray for him. That's how humble the Heflins were. "Pray for the blood to stop," he said.

We prayed a simple prayer. Then he took a handkerchief and tied it around that hand to keep the wound clean and went back to work. The Heflins never used Band-aids or antibiotic salves. They prayed, and that was it. The wound healed quickly, but it left a scar on the top of his hand. He told me several times through the years that he loved that scar because when he laid hands on the sick to pray, he could remember what God had done for him that day.

ONE LORD OF THE HARVEST

There is Someone who is Lord of the harvest, and it's not you. It's not your overseer, your bishop, or some other higher up. It's also not your spouse. There is one Lord of the Harvest, and His name is Jesus.

So what should we do? The people around us too often fail to appreciate our gifts. They cannot look inside of you and see the seed that is growing there, and therefore they don't give you the opportunities you need to grow. This is one of the greatest sins of our day. Pastors are concerned with getting more and more members, while the members they already have are not given the opportunity for their gifts and abilities in God to grow.

We have classes designed for tiny children and classes designed for those of increasing age. Once a person reaches a certain level of maturity, we feel that they shouldn't need any further classes. But we all need to continue growing. There are wonderful things in us that need to come out, and we need to do whatever it takes to get them developed so that we can be used to our full potential in the Kingdom of God.

Other people often fail to appreciate what we have to offer. When we do have a chance to minister, they often fail to give us the encouragement we need to move forward and go higher and deeper in God. But even if you fail to get any encouragement from people, it doesn't matter.

It doesn't matter if the people you minister to think to give you a wonderful love offering or not. It is wonderful to minister and be applauded and rewarded, but it is just as wonderful to minister when there is no applause and no monetary reward. Let it be, to you, just the same. If you will do it, not for the applause or the love offering, but rather for the Kingdom's sake and for the Lord of the harvest, you will never be disappointed.

When you recognize Him as Lord of the harvest and obey Him, fitting in where He needs you to fit in and accomplishing the specific task or tasks that He needs you to accomplish, then you will be blessed. And all your needs will be supplied.

Miraculous Ministry Facilities in Ecuador

While I was living in Ecuador, for many years we enjoyed the free use of a wonderful campground. People came from all over South America to be filled with the Spirit, receive the gifts of the Spirit, and go back to bless their own people. After more than six years, the owner of the facility decided to do something else with it, and we suddenly had nowhere to house our many families and our many ministries.

We had a team of fifty that we had developed. Some were Americans, but there were also many Ecuadorians and some Colombians and Venezuelans. As I prayed about where we should go, the Lord spoke to me to go see an Ecuadorian pastor named Zenon Rivera. I knew Pastor Rivera, but not very well. What I had heard about him was that he had a great heart and a great vision.

As Pastor Rivera's story unfolded, it was truly amazing. A businessman, he had been led to start a church in his home some years before. That small congregation had grown until it needed a building of its own. The men of the church had banded together, purchased a property, and erected a building. It lacked a lot of finishing touches, but the structures were there.

Amazingly, the congregation had built, not only a very nice sanctuary and some Sunday school rooms (as most churches do); they had also built extra floors and extra rooms because the Lord had told them they would have a Christian book store, a Bible school, a tract ministry, radio and television programs, and much more. This was a lot for a congregation of about sixty people to contemplate. When I was led to go see Pastor Zenon, I knew none of this.

We talked, and I told him what had happened to us and that we were now looking for a place to relocate to. We not only had our people; we had many ministries. We had our Bible School, we had our Christian book distribution, we had our tract printing ministry, we had our radio programs, etc. And we would need some rooms to serve as our office.

Tears came to his eyes, and he said to me, "I have a small board of faithful men and women who have agreed to help me pray and know the mind of God on future decisions for the church. Would you be willing to meet with them and to tell them exactly what you have told me?" I told him I would be very happy to do that, and a meeting was arranged for a couple of nights later.

I took several of our people with me that night, so there were other witnesses to what happened next. The group received us warmly, and the pastor asked me if I would repeat what I had been telling him at his home only days before. As I began to speak, I couldn't help but notice that tears were forming in the eyes of the entire group. I wasn't sure what was happening, but God was doing something wonderful.

As soon as I had finished, the brothers said to us, "Please, come with us. We have something to show you." Someone pulled out a key ring and went ahead of us down the various hallways, opening rooms for us to enter and view.

The rooms were not elegant in any sense of the word. Most of them were still unpainted, but they had walls and floors, doors, and windows. "Would this room work for the Bible school?" we were asked. "Would this one work for the tract ministry?" "I think this room would make a nice office." And this went on and on. It was a three-storey building, and two entire floors of it were dedicated to rooms that were now being offered for our ministries.

Who Would Be in Charge?

As great a miracle as this all was, it is always tense joining with others in such a work. Who would be in charge? Who would make vital decisions? Pastor Zenon told me he thought I should be the pastor and the others would serve under me. As I prayed about it, God told me to leave him as pastor. I would work at his side. And that's what we did. In those rooms we developed offices, conference rooms, a recording studio, Bible, tract, and book storage, etc., and downstairs on the main level, we put in a Christian book store.

Until we could find enough housing, some of our people even lived in that building. Before long, we added a fourth floor to the main building where we housed and fed the Bible school students.

OUT OF SPACE AGAIN

After a few years, we ran out of space again and decided to add another smaller, three-storey building on the side. This one had to be built from scratch, and it was an education for me to see how such a building was constructed in that part of the world. There were no concrete trucks, no concrete pumps, and no jacks to hold up the concrete forms for each new level. The forms were all built by hand, and the concrete was all mixed, moved, and poured by hand.

The most difficult part was pouring the slab itself on each level. It had to be done in one day, for there could be no seams. To accomplish this, we called all of the Bible school students and teachers to work alongside the pastors and volunteers from among the members, and we were all there ready to get started early one Saturday morning.

Understanding the Seed

A Complex and Backbreaking Process

The process was complex. Two men carried between them a wooden box with long handles on it. It was first filled with sand from a pile at the street. They took it to an open area between the buildings where the mixing was to be done and dumped it on a concreted patio area. Then they went back for more. Next came the gravel and finally a bag of cement was brought and dumped on top of the mix. Once this was all mixed, they were ready for the water.

Since it took a while to get enough materials together in that spot to start the mixing, several worked on this process of moving the materials. Then, as the process got moving, some of them were able to transfer to the mixing (done by hand with short shovels). To get everyone busy, several jumped in and worked on the mixing at first, doing it as fast as they could because a team was ready with buckets to start handing the mix up the crude scaffolding.

Pouring the Third Level

Most memorable to me was the pouring of the third floor. We needed a man on each level, and buckets were handed up from one level to the next to the next. The person receiving the bucket on the top level then had to carry it to the particular spot that was being poured at the moment and dump it out. Another person was there to work the concrete down into the form. As this all got underway, there was great joy and excitement, and everyone was singing and praising the Lord as they worked.

It was a wonderfully infectious atmosphere, but it wasn't hard to see that this was going to be a long and difficult day. It was a big form, it required a lot of concrete, and it all had to be mixed and poured in this painstaking way, and it had to be finished in one day. Whew! What a day it was to be!

In the first couple of hours, everything went beautifully, and it seemed that we could easily complete the job in one day. Then, however, some began to tire. Sand is heavy, gravel is heavy, and once the two of them are mixed with cement and water, the resulting mix is VERY heavy.

Not only was this a never-ending process; if one person failed to do his job, everyone down the line (or up the line, in this case) was stalled, and nothing was being accomplished. When I saw it the first time, a terrible feeling came over me, almost like a panic. If we could not keep up our pace, the work would not get done in time. This could ruin everything for the new building. What should I do? I prayed, and the Lord showed me that I should move to the weak area and take up the slack.

Take Up the Slack

The first tiredness seemed to manifest in those who were mixing, so I put someone in my place, dropped down the scaffolding, and picked up a shovel. "Let me help you, brothers," I said. "That's hard work." That was an understatement. It was backbreaking work. But now I jumped in and began mixing with all I was worth, speaking words of encouragement as I did. "We can do this, in the name of Jesus." This got the line moving again and gave one brother a chance to catch his breath, get a drink of water, and come back refreshed.

When the tiredness appeared in the line of buckets being lifted up, I moved there to help out until someone got their second wind. In this way, as the day progressed, I served in many positions. I did what needed to be done. That evening, we were all very tired, but we were also very happy. We had gotten the job done for God.

I never forgot the events of that day because this concept came to signify for me the secret of successful ministry, of accomplishment, of obedience to God. He is the Lord of the harvest, and I must be where He most needs me at any particular moment. If, for some reason, the entire kitchen staff at Calvary Campground went on strike, I guarantee that Sister Jane Lowder would be in there cooking, and some of us would be in there helping her do it.

Fit in where you are needed. Go where God needs you in His harvest field. Do what He needs you to do at any particular moment.

How Can You Know?

How can you know where you should be and what you should be doing? There is only one Lord of the harvest, and while it is a good thing to be responsive to those who are over you (and you will surely be blessed if you are), there is One to whom you will ultimately answer. He knows it when you are rebellious toward others or toward Him.

When others cannot tell us what we should be doing, we must not be disturbed by that. Know that the Lord of the harvest can tell you. He knows better than anyone else, and He can show you where the weak point is. He can show you people who desperately need your prayers and will respond to your ministry. He can also show you those who only want to consume your time and are seemingly unwilling to change, and you can avoid them. He will show you where the investment of your time in His Kingdom will produce the most fruit.

Never Forget!

Please never forget that you are a worker for the Lord. That's why I don't like the modern custom of giving everyone titles. We're all just workers together with Him.

What was His final word to the Corinthians and to us?

> *Therefore, my beloved brethren, be steadfast, immovable, always abounding in the work of the Lord, knowing that your labor is not in vain in the Lord.*
>
> 1 Corinthians 15:50-58

When Sarah Jane Lowder had to cut down trees and chop fire wood because many of the men who were volunteering for the camp didn't know how to use a chain saw or an axe, that labor was not in vain. That's the reason she is the director of that great ministry today. Whatever she was needed for, that's what she did, and she did it faithfully and cheerfully.

There may have been more talented people. There may have been more brilliant people. There may have been more intellectual people. There definitely were richer people. But there were no more dedicated and faithful people. Jane Lowder is director of that ministry today because wherever the need was in the Kingdom, she stepped into that need and did the job.

ANYTIME DAY OR NIGHT

I was visiting the camp once, and I noticed that after we had all returned to the camp from having a night service in the Richmond church, the camp staff members were going quickly to their rooms and then coming back out in work clothes. It was already late at night. They had worked all day and then gone to church that night, and yet they were back to work some more because a certain building had to be finished in time for campmeeting. Hungry people would be coming to seek God, and they needed a comfortable place to stay. That's the dedication that built Calvary Campground. Those people worked well past midnight, but the result was that God sent them to the nations.

Never lose sight of the fact that the work of the Lord is WORK. People work hard in their secular jobs to make a living and provide for their families. Can it be right for those of us who call ourselves servants of God to sit around and talk all day or do whatever we want? God's Kingdom is work, and no labor for that Kingdom is in vain or will go unrewarded.

Amen!

CHAPTER 5

GOING TO THE OTHER SIDE
BY LADY JANE LOWDER

There were many wonderful things done at Calvary Campground before I ever came on the scene. Unfortunately, I never met Wallace Heflin, Sr., and I've not even heard one of his messages, except for a little bit of one tape recording, and it was not a very good recording. But I've heard many wonderful stories of his faith, how he motivated people, and how he trusted and believed God — he and Sister Edith Heflin. We are the heirs of their sowing, and God is still doing wonderful things at the camp today. He is so good.

WHAT CAMP WAS LIKE

When I came to the camp, it didn't look like it does today. It was still very rustic. There was a gravel-covered dirt road leading into the place, and all of the areas between buildings was either grassy or just dirt.

The floor of the camp tabernacle was dirt with some gravel over it. At the front of that building, some remnants of carpet had been pieced together to cover the ground and provide a more comfortable place for people to pray. Those remnants were of many different colors. They were also of different sizes, so they overlapped each other in a crazy-quilt pattern that was a nightmare to clean. There was no vacuum cleaner, so those carpets had to be swept by hand with a broom each morning and then adjusted so that they fit together in the best possible way.

None of the old theater seats were attached to the ground, and if a seat was rocked the wrong way, the whole row would fall over.

Every morning we went to prayer in the small prayer room. It was the very first building erected on the campground and served for many years as the Ashland Church.

That building was heated by a small wood stove, and there was also a wood stove in the kitchen, but no other building was heated at the time. The dining room was used in the winter months for storage and was filled with every imaginable thing.

Brother Wallace Heflin, Jr. would go to the front every morning after the handful of us who stayed here at the time had finished our hour of prayer, give us some instructions about what needed to be done that day, and then encourage us to do our best.

"They're Coming"

I arrived at camp on June 16, 1976, and that next day, in my first prayer meeting, Brother Heflin got up and said, "Well, they're coming, so we have to get everything ready!"

I thought to myself, "Who's coming? And where are they coming from?" The place was in the backwoods, in the countryside.

In Ashland itself, there were no fast-food restaurants yet, and there was only one grocery store, an A&P. There was a gas station, and there was one place where you could buy a pair of shoes, but shopping in Ashland, Virginia was still very limited.

There were already a few houses along the road that passes by the camp, but most of the rest of the area was still wooded. So where were all these people coming from? It was a mystery to me.

No Place Prepared for Us

When I arrived the previous afternoon, accompanied by another sister from Sanford, North Carolina, we were sure that, since they knew we were coming, there would be a place prepared for us to sleep. We were wrong. When we were told where we would sleep, we went to see it and couldn't believe our eyes.

The room was still filled with stored items from winter. We had to first get all of that out and find a place for it. Then, once that was out, we discovered that the walls of the room were covered with mildew, and we had to begin scrubbing them. This took us all afternoon. Pastor friends from Sanford, Lloyd and Mayline Ashby, had brought us, and when Sister Mayline saw the condition of the place we were going to have to stay, she wept. She loved the campground, but she wondered how we could live under such conditions. I was just happy and excited to be there. Once we had our room in livable condition, then we were ready to get to work, and there was plenty for us to do.

"Take Charge of the Dish Room"

Very early on Mother Heflin told me that she felt I should take charge of the dish room. That was not something I wanted to hear. I hadn't come to camp to wash dishes. I had just quit restaurant work, and I had been the manager, with some fifteen people working under me. I had started working as a teenager in a dish room, but that had now been a long time ago. But Mother Heflin was in charge of the campground, so I had to revert back to washing dishes. My job was more than that, of course. I was also to be part of all that was going on in the kitchen and dining room.

"Take a Little Walk with Me"

The first morning, Sister Heflin came to me and said, "I'd like for you to take a little walk with me." There were a couple of other sisters who were also invited to take this walk. We all followed her into the kitchen, not knowing what to expect.

She approached one of the big freezers, lifted the lid, and looked inside. There were about ten or twelve loaves of bread in it, probably several days old already. She lifted her hands to the Lord and said, "Sweet Jesus, precious Jesus, I love You, and You never fail."

It was such a simple prayer that I could hardly believe it, but that was the way she prayed. "Oh, Jesus," she continued, we have people coming, so I ask You to fill this freezer. Fill it so that we can feed Your people." And then she moved on to the next freezer and did the same thing.

From the freezers, we moved on to the cupboards (which had nothing in them), and prayed over each of them, believing God that He would fill them to feed all the people who were coming. It was all new and strange to me, but I never forgot it.

She was never overly loud, she never screamed, and she never beat the air with her fists. She knew what she needed, and she asked God to supply it. She trusted Him to fulfill His Word in her life. What a wonderful beginning that was for me, walking with her and seeing those miracles, for the freezers and the cupboards soon began to fill up, and we somehow always had enough to feed those who came. During the next sixteen days until campmeeting opened, I saw miracle after miracle, and the miracles I didn't see I heard about.

The Heflins Loved to Tell Miracle Stories

The favorite thing of the Heflins, all of them, was to talk about miracles. Brother Heflin loved to tell us about the miracles God had done for him in Argentina, the Philippines, or some other country where he had traveled and ministered. Or it might be something Sister Ruth had done or his mom or dad had done. They lived miracles, and every single day of our lives we heard their stories of miracles.

They loved to tell about how God moved and how He supplied, how He made a way where there was no way, and this was our diet three hundred and sixty-five days a year. One of the foods we never missed a day getting was a story of a miracle God had done.

WE SAW MANY MIRACLES FOR OURSELVES

That year we saw many great and wonderful miracles for ourselves. For instance, one young man who was helping around the camp took the radiator cap off of a vehicle before the engine had cooled enough, and the hot fluid spurted out all over him. When they tried to take off his shirt to see how badly he was burned, the skin came off with it.

Someone ran and got Brother Heflin, and he came and laid that big hand on the boy and prayed over him. God took out the pain, and he never went to a doctor. Nowadays that absolutely blows people's minds, but it's true. The wound healed up, and he was as good as new.

Another of the miracles that happened that first year was for me personally. I was splitting wood by Mother Heflin's house, and one piece had a knot in it, which caused the axe to glance off of it, a piece of wood flew off and hit me near my eye, and blood gushed out of the wound.

I saw David Henderson walking across the grounds, so I called to him and asked him to come and help me. As he approached, he said, "Oh! My God, you're bleeding!"

I said, "Yeah, the axe glanced off, so a chip came off and hit me in my face." He laid hands on me and prayed, and the wound instantly stopped bleeding.

I went into one of the camp rest rooms, washed the blood off of my face, and went back to work. But no sooner had I hit the same piece of wood than the very same thing happened again. This time the wood chip hit me on the other side of my face. Since God had healed me the first time, I knew He would do it again. And He did.

Learning Fasting

There was a lady on the campground that first year named Sister Correta, and she was on a forty-day fast, and the woman sang all day long. She sang through the morning, sang through the afternoon, and was still singing when night came. I was very doubtful about the fasting thing. How could someone fast for so many days? So I watched every move she made.

Even though she was fasting (or so she said), she worked all day every day. She worked in the dining hall, and she worked down at the tabernacle, putting down carpet, and she was singing the whole time. One day I said to her, "Could I come to your room for a while and just talk to you?"

She said, "Yes, sure. That would be wonderful." She didn't know that I had invited myself to her room because I wanted to look around, absolutely sure that I would find some food there. It was just hard for me to believe that anyone could go forty days without eating. Much to my surprise, there was no food at all in her room.

In those days, nobody on the campground kept food in their room. Nobody had a refrigerator, and nobody had a hotpot. The rooms were bare, with the exception of Shirley Garland's room. Because she had a small boy (Glenn is still part of the camp family today), so they were permitted to have a hotpot. But she was the only one.

There were four of us crowded into a small room, so there wasn't much space to move about, but it was all wonderful because we were seeing miracle after miracle.

SISTER CORRETA'S THUMB

Sister Correta was down at the tabernacle one day, putting down some carpet on the platform, and somehow she accidentally hit her thumb and tore the nail practically off. She came up to the snack bar where I was working.

At the time, the snack bar was just a small room with an open area attached. The area where the people sat consisted of five or six tables on the bare ground, and it was all surrounded by chicken wire, nothing else.

I saw Sister Correta coming holding her thumb. She asked if I would pray for her. I looked at the thumb and could see that the nail was torn nearly off. I took hold of it and began to pray. When I had finished, she pulled her thumb back and looked at it and said, "All the pain is gone."

That should have made me very happy, but I was so new at prayer that it actually frightened me. Wow! Her pain was gone. I shouldn't have been surprised because I asked Jesus to take the pain, and He did it. She left and went back to work.

I Got Healed Too

For years one of my feet turned out when I walked because I had something wrong with my hip. That hip would sometimes pop out of joint, and when it happened, it was very painful. Something about the hip also caused the foot to turn out. Now, as I was going down a path that led to our rooms, I laid my hand on that hip and prayed, "God, why don't You heal my hip someday?" If I could lay hands on a throbbing thumb with the nail practically torn off and all the pain went away instantly, then I felt sure that God could heal me at some point.

I hadn't asked Him to do it that instant, and I wasn't expecting it to be done right then and there, but no sooner had I uttered that prayer than I felt something move inside my hip (something twisted), and from that day to this my hip has never gone out of joint again. That hip was now straight, and my foot no longer turned out.

These were the beginnings of miracles, of seeing miracles, of having miracles explained to us, of receiving miracles, and of doing miracles. Oh, it was so totally exciting to be here in such a miracle place.

My First Campmeeting

Campmeeting was about to start, and everybody was very excited. I was excited just to be a part of it, and I didn't care what I was asked to do. I hadn't come to camp because I didn't have a home or I didn't have money, and I hadn't come because I didn't have a job. I had come because God had spoken to me and told me to come. I thought it was just for the days of preparation and the four weeks of summer camptime, but He knew that it would turn into a lifetime of miracles.

That first night of campmeeting I was amazed at how many people had come, and they were from everywhere. Sister Ruth Ward Heflin was always the opening campmeeting speaker, and so she preached those first two weeks. The meetings were absolutely wonderful and exciting.

That first night I saw several hundred people get up out of their seats and start running around the tabernacle at once. I saw people weeping. I saw people lying on their faces on the ground. They were dirty and sweaty, and dust clouds swirled above their heads. Those dust clouds were thick, but the cloud of glory that covered us all was even thicker. It was all so wonderful.

Attendance Was a Requirement

The next day I went to the 11 A.M. service, in which Mother Heflin was ministering. I didn't really have a choice because it was a requirement. Attendance at night was also a requirement, no matter how many hours we had put into keeping everyone fed and keeping the campgrounds and buildings clean. There were certain chores that kept some few camp people out of the service, but these were always kept at a minimum, and if you had not been assigned one of those particular chores, you were expected to be there.

Just being there was not also enough. You were expected to be attentive and to participate in the service, no matter how tired you might feel.

My Lovely Camp Dress and My Unruly Hair

Just before campmeeting opened, I was told that I would be sitting on the platform. It amazed me that they would ask someone like me to sit on the platform. In fact, I was embarrassed to be up there, not knowing why I was there. At the same time, they gave me a dress to wear. There was an official camp dress, and everybody had to have one, so we all dressed alike. The problem was that the dress they gave me was several sizes too large, and I looked like a sack of potatoes in it.

Another problem was my hair. Just two weeks before coming to camp I'd had very long hair. When working in the restaurant I had to keep it up, but one day it came undone and fell down while I was working, and I decided that it was time get it cut. I went out that very afternoon to have it cut, and I asked for it to be cut short.

The lady I had gone to had serious reservations about cutting my beautiful hair (especially cutting it so short), and she walked away three times before she could do it. Each time she asked, "Are you sure you want it cut so short? I have to go do something, and I want you to think about it while I'm away."

I thought about it, and when she came back, I said, "I still want to have it cut." It was an extreme change, from being very long to being very short, but I thought that was what I wanted. I was a serious worker, and long hair got in my way. She finally cut it, and she cut it VERY SHORT. It didn't take her long at all.

By the time I moved to Calvary Campground, the hair had grown out a little, enough to put it in an Afro, and that's what I had when I came here. But here all the women wore their hair up. I tried to get my hair up, but there just wasn't enough of it to work with. I had worn it up all my life, but now fixing it that way was a problem. I must have used fifty bobby pins trying to hold it all up. God, in His mercy and His grace, helped me get through those days and be able to go forth to the future He had in store for me.

Going to Israel

That fall, after campmeeting had ended and our work on the grounds was finished for the season, I went to Israel. That was the beginning of many years of wonderful travel to the nations and some great things that God was about to do in my life.

Why am I saying all of this? When the Lord puts you in a place, stay there until He has finished with you in that place. You will be stretched in any place He puts you, no matter where it is or what He shows you to do there. If there is no stretching, there is no growing. You must be stretched if you are to grow in the Lord.

I stayed in the camp dishroom for the next twenty-two years, but during that time I travelled the world over in the months we didn't have campmeeting. I would be gone six to eight months at a time, and I would preach and have large meetings in many countries. Then I would come back to camp and go back into that dish room and pick up where I had left off.

Not Many Opportunities

Did I get many opportunities to preach at camp itself? No, in those early years, I didn't. I felt blessed when I was given fifteen minutes in some service to tell about what God had done for me during the past six months. That was a lot to tell in such a short time, but beyond all of that, God was working something wonderful in my life, and it really didn't matter whether someone ever asked me to tell what God had done in and through me. I knew, and He never forgets. In fact, He has it all written down. Those foundational years were so important and so wonderful.

Going Around the World on $70

In 1979 three of us camp ladies were believing God to take us on a ministry trip around the world. We didn't have any money when we decided to make the trip, but God began to give us some. Even before we had it all, Brother Heflin helped us to get our ticket through Wayne Lawhorn (a good brother who owned a Richmond travel agency that helped missionaries get the best prices), and we were able to charge the balance to be paid later.

Somewhere along the way, I got my money together, but one of the other sisters did not have hers, so I gave her half of my money so that she could pay half of her fare. So we each paid half, and we charged the rest. Brother Heflin, of course, was standing behind us, praying with us and believing God for miracles, and allowing us to do what God had called us to do.

We left here with a little more than $70.00 each in spending money. That wasn't much, considering that we didn't know anyone in the places we felt led to go. We really didn't know what we were going to do, where we would end up, or any other details. All we knew was that God had spoken to us to go to certain countries.

Receiving Some Offerings

After leaving camp, we went to Tennessee and spoke in a church there, and they gave us an offering. We sent the money back to Brother Heflin to be paid on our tickets.

We went on to California where we had a friend, Sister Winnie. We spoke for her, she gave us an offering, and we sent the money back to Brother Heflin to pay on our tickets.

From California, we flew to Hawaii. We didn't know anyone there, so when we arrived at the Honolulu Airport, we found a phone book, prayed over it, and asked God to show us where we were to go. We opened the phone book and began to look through the list of area churches. We felt that God showed us a place called Prayer Mountain.

After we decided that this was where the Lord was sending us, Debbie Jones had a vision. She saw a long table, and she saw the head of the table, and the plate at the head of the table was turned upside down. She said, "Sister Jane, the head of this place is not going to be there." We decided to go anyway, and, sure enough, when we got there, the head of that group had just left. Not only had he left; he had left abruptly and never came back. It was amazing. God knows everything.

We stayed with the people of Prayer Mountain for a few days, and they invited us to speak at one of their home fellowships on the Sunday before we were to leave. We spoke that Sunday, and they gave us a wonderful offering. We sent it back to Brother Heflin to pay on our tickets.

So, when we left Honolulu and departed from U.S. airspace, headed for Korea, Japan, China, Hong Kong, the Philippines, India, and Nepal, we still only had about $73 each, but God was about to bless us in new ways.

Miracles in Taiwan

By the time we got to Taiwan our money was running low. Before the trip, I had never heard of airport taxes, but I learned quickly. Sometimes it was a choice between airport taxes and eating. If we didn't have money for airport taxes, we couldn't go anywhere. We now had enough only for one or two nights in a hotel.

We weren't sure what to do, so we walked the streets of Taipei for the next seven hours, praying and believing God to guide us and provide for us. "You told us to come," we reminded Him, "now what do You want us to do here?"

We did have a contact someone had given us, the phone number of a pastor, and we had called that number from Hawaii, but the communication was very strained. I understood the person who answered to say that the man was no longer a pastor.

After praying for those seven hours, we got a room for the night and then tried that number again. This time a lady who spoke better English answered. She told us that the pastor was in a far mountain place praying. She put another lady on the phone, and this lady said they would call us back within a few minutes.

She called and said, "We are having a service in the church tonight. Somebody will come by to pick you up, and Pastor wants you to share a testimony with us." So that night, each of us shared a short testimony.

Sharing Our Testimonies

We had been taught by Brother Heflin that if someone invited us to give a testimony, we were not to take over the service. Instead, we were to give a short, but powerful testimony that glorified Jesus. And that is just what we intended to do.

I let the other ladies go first, and I gave my testimony last. I was led to tell the people how God had touched my life and healed me and how we were now able to go around the world for Him. When I finished, God gave me two words of knowledge about people there. I first called out a word of knowledge over someone's back, and when I did, that person fell out of their chair under the Spirit. Then God gave me another word, and that person was powerfully touched as well. The assistant pastor came to us and said, "Please, would you take the whole service?" We took the service that night, and every person in that place, except for three, received the baptism of the Holy Spirit and spoke in tongues. It was a new beginning.

Three More Days?

The pastor called me that night and asked if we would be willing to stay for three more days, just to speak to and encourage the church. The problem was that we didn't have enough money left to stay in the hotel for three days, so I said to him, "Let me ask the others."

I cupped my hand over the phone, so that he couldn't hear what I was saying, and I asked the other ladies what they thought we should do. They both answered, "Whatever the Lord says to you, we'll do it."

That was all I needed to hear. I said to him, "Okay. We're going to stay." We talked a little while longer and then hung up.

"Now, get up," I said to my companions. "We need to pray. We need a miracle." It was already midnight, but we started praying. About twenty minutes later, the phone rang again. It was the pastor. He said, "I forgot to tell you that you don't have to worry about anything. We'll take care of your hotel, we'll take care of your food, and we'll take care of your transportation. All we want you to do is minister to the church and to our students." God was working for us.

Seven More Days?

We did the meetings for the next three days, and then a prophetic word came forth to us: "God is speaking to you to stay seven more days." Staying on, however, could not be our decision; it had to come from the pastor. He immediately got up from where he was, came over to us, and asked, "Are you willing to do what the Lord is telling you?"

I didn't hesitate this time. I immediately answered, "Yes." So we stayed for seven more days.

Then another prophetic word came forth, and we extended our stay again. We were in that place a total of two months, and during that time, we went all over Taiwan, transported by motorcycles, all three of us going different directions and having meetings every night and every morning.

We received wonderful offerings in Taiwan, so that when we left there we had more money than we'd had when we left home. Because God had called us to go and we had obeyed, He had also supplied. He made a way.

That pastor opened doors for us to preach and teach the Gospel among the Chinese in many other places — in other areas of Taiwan, but also in Australia, the Philippines, Singapore, Indonesia, and the islands — wherever Chinese people had settled.

I Still Didn't Feel Like a Preacher

In all of this, I never felt like I was a preacher. I had been sent to tell anyone who was willing to listen of God's goodness. I knew that He had saved me, He had healed me, and He had called me. He had anointed me, filling me with His Holy Spirit, and I was only too glad to go and tell others what He had done for me. If He had done it for me, I knew that He was willing to do it for others as well. There are no limits when we believe God and do His will.

Will we ever feel that we are capable of going and doing His work? Probably not. But the Christ in us is more than sufficient to empower us to go forth and do what we cannot do in ourselves.

If we could do it all ourselves, God would not be glorified. So He always gives us something to do that we could not do otherwise. It takes His wisdom, His knowledge, and His understanding for us to be able to accomplish the great things He has called each of us to do. And He has indeed called us to do great things.

You may not know yet what it is that God has called you to accomplish in this life, but you will learn. However, let me warn you: When you are careful to please God and do His will, not everyone will like you for it. Get used to that fact. Then surrender your all to Him willingly and wholeheartedly, for there are thousands waiting to hear from you. They will like you. In fact, they will absolutely love you.

Preaching at Camp for the First Time

In 1997 Sister Ruth Heflin asked me, for the first time, to be one of the campmeeting speakers that year. She said that God had spoken to her that I should do it. The very thought of it scared me to death and literally made me want to run away. In one sense I was thrilled, but in another sense I was terrified. What should I do?

To add to my fears, some of those who lived on camp at the time were not happy with the fact that I had been chosen to do this (and not them). Why me? I could see their point.

I was walking across the yard one day, and I prayed desperately, "God, they're totally against me."

He answered me, "And I'm totally for you."

Then He repeated it: "I'm totally for you."

Well, if God is totally for you, then it doesn't matter who else is against you. His Word says, *"If God be for us, who can be against us?"* (Romans 8:31).

I Want to Tell You the Same Thing

I want to tell you the same thing today. It doesn't matter what others might say about you. If God is for you, who can be against you? You can rise up, and you can be and do what He has called you to be and do. As the Scriptures declare:

> *Not by might, nor by power, but by my spirit, saith the* L ORD *of hosts.*   Zechariah 4:6

In Him and through Him, you can be and you can do whatever He calls you to be and do.

He doesn't promise that there won't be problems along the way. He doesn't say there won't be storms. He doesn't tell you that everything will be rosy and beautiful in life. But He does promise:

> *No weapon that is formed against thee shall prosper; and every tongue that shall rise against thee in judgment thou shalt condemn. This is the heritage of the servants of the Lord, and their righteousness is of me, saith the* Lord.
> Isaiah 54:17

> *And call upon me in the day of trouble: I will deliver thee, and thou shalt glorify me.*   Psalm 50:15

God is for you, no matter what else is going on at the moment. When He called you, He already knew His plan for you, and He will not let go until that plan becomes reality in your life.

Are You Tired?

We sometimes get tired and decide that we don't want to go on. We may sit down, feel sorry for ourselves, cry a little, and wish we were somewhere else. Sometimes we even wish that Jesus would come quickly.

He will let you do all that, but then He will say, "Get up now and go on. There is no place for sitting still in My Kingdom, no place for not doing."

You may say, "But I don't know the next step." That's okay. He does, and He'll help you.

While Jesus was here on the earth, everything He said was training for His disciples, and now He's training you. In fact, He's been training some of you for many years now, and you haven't yet arrived. That's okay. Stay in the training. You'll get there.

The Disciple in Training

Jesus' disciples were also in training:

Now it came to pass on a certain day, that he went into a ship with his disciples: and he said unto them, Let us go over unto the other side of the lake. And they launched forth. Luke 8:22

I love this verse. Jesus had been doing some wonderful things, and His disciples were blessed to be a part of it. They had learned how wonderful it is to walk with Him. As they traveled together, He was talking to many others, but He also had intimate times with them when He spoke directly to their needs.

On this particular day, *"He said unto them ... ."* Thank God that He is still speaking to His disciples today, and you and I are those disciples. We are His ministers. We are His hands. We are His eyes. We are those who must represent Him in His fullness. We are His representatives, we are the expression of His goodness in the earth, and we are the lights of the world. It is not because we chose to be or could be of our own accord, but because He has put His light in us. Since He is the Light of the world, we are now that light.

God has called us, and most of us have heard His call and turned aside to follow after Him. I'm not talking about giving up everything you have or leaving your job to do something else. I'm talking about hearing God's voice, knowing that He is calling you, and deciding to walk with Him.

We might not know what the next day will bring, but it doesn't matter because we know Him who has called us, and we trust Him and believe that He will take care of us. We have confidence that He will protect us. He will feed us. He will clothe us. He will help us in every way. He will strengthen us. He will give us wisdom, knowledge, and understanding, not just once a week, but throughout every single day.

God will give you whatever you need at the moment. He has said:

If any of you lack wisdom, let him ask of God, that giveth to all men liberally, and upbraideth not; and it shall be given him. James 1:5

This promised *wisdom* is godly wisdom, and He will drop it into your spirit in the very moment you most need it.

They Got into the Boat

Jesus and the disciples got into that boat and started for the other side, and they were in the perfect will of God in doing so. But just because you are walking in the perfect will of God does not mean that no storms will be coming your way. It does not mean that no adverse winds will blow upon you. It does not mean that something will not happen that will seem to adversely affect the course of your day.

Storms will come. You cannot avoid them. Difficulties will come. You cannot avoid them. You can pray, and you can believe God for certain things, but know that you will be opposed. Also know that when something does happen that seems to threaten your future, if you will turn to the Lord, look to Him, and surrender yourself to Him, He will help you.

This wonderful story helps me. If Peter, James, and John encountered storms when they were doing what Jesus had told them to do, then who am I not to expect them in my life too? If their training included fierce storms, then I can surely expect some.

The Storms Did Not End

The storms in the lives of the disciples of Jesus did not end when they had safely come to the other side that day. They were still experiencing storms even after He had given His life for them. Their storms continued on the other side of the cross. Even after Jesus had risen from the dead and ascended up to Heaven, trials and persecutions continued for His followers, but they had learned what to do. They could handle storms because Jesus was with them.

Going to the Other Side

Jesus Slept

When they had set sail the day described in Luke 8, Jesus found a place to curl up, and He soon went to sleep. He was tired, for He had been ministering for a long time. He was still sleeping when the storm arose, and the winds picked up on the lake and beat against the boat they were in ... until it began filling with water, and their lives were suddenly in jeopardy.

Now these men knew how to handle a boat, and they knew that lake very well. They had fished it many times, in good weather and bad. But they also knew how quickly a deadly storm could come up and put them all in peril. And this one was bad. For them to cry out as they did, having weathered so many storms in the past, it must have been fierce indeed:

> *And they came to him, and awoke him, saying, Master, master, we perish.*   Luke 8:24

These men knew how badly Jesus needed His rest, and they would not have awakened Him unnecessarily. They were not accustomed to overreacting to the sea. This was a very real threat. Their lives were all in danger.

Don't Hesitate to Call Out for Help

In the midst of your storm, don't be afraid to call out to Jesus. Your prayer might be: "Master, I feel like I'm dying!" or, "Master, I don't know how I got into this mess, and I don't know how to get out of it. I need Your help," or some such sentiment. That's okay.

Mark recorded these words from the disciples' mouths:

Master, carest thou not that we perish?   Mark 4:38

Well, that, at least, *was* an overreaction. We know that He *did* care, and He was willing to wake up and help them. The disciples were desperate and didn't know what else to do. They had done everything they knew to do, and nothing was working. In desperation now, they cried to Jesus, and He *"arose."*

JESUS AROSE

Then he arose, and rebuked the wind and the raging of the water: and they ceased, and there was a calm.
Luke 8:24

Asleep, Jesus did not appear to be so powerful, but now He *"arose,"* and when He did, His power was evident. He was the sovereign God, the Windbreaker, the Storm Chaser, and He still is. He is your Stronghold, your Refuge, and All that you need. *"He rebuked the wind and the raging of the water, and they ceased and there was a calm."* When we are going through our difficult places, we can know that He alone can bring us the peace and calmness that we so desperately need.

Sometimes a storm can still be raging around us, but because He has rebuked it, we already feel a peace and calm on the inside. In those moments, we can know that no matter what is happening, no matter what the circumstances look like, no matter how things feel to us, no matter what the elements are saying, we can feel a confidence and total peace on the inside and know that God is in control and will work it all out.

SPINNING OUT OF CONTROL

When a storm comes in the natural, we usually know what to do. In preparation, we must brace weak things. We must get into the safest area of a structure. We must prepare or cover windows. We must have emergency supplies, etc., but sometimes storms come suddenly and unexpectedly, and that can cause panic to rise up within us, and we can't think straight and don't know what to do.

Some storms can be so threatening that it seems that our whole world is spinning out of control. In that very critical moment, we can hear the sweet voice of the Holy Spirit speaking to us, and if we do, a calmness will take control of us and help us to think right and know what is the proper action to take.

Storms, any of them, are no match for Jesus. He arose and rebuked the winds and the raging of the waters, and they ceased, and there was a calm. And He is with you today in the very same way. You may have felt His call to get into His boat and cross over, and then the storm suddenly arose. Your storm may be financial. It may just be emotional. Your own mind might be telling you that you can't make it, you can't do it:

"This is too big for you."
"There are too many against you."
"Nobody likes you."

It is often our own minds that make us restless and afraid. We imagine the worst, when God wants to give us His best.

Let a calmness come to your spirit today. Let all raging cease. Hear His voice speaking to the winds and waves. Rest in Him. If He told you to go to the other side, you can make it. You *will* make it.

Not Just a Onetime Experience

Going to the other side is not just a onetime experience. One day it involves our families, another day it involves our finances, and another day it may involve a nation God has placed on our hearts. Whatever He tells you to do, expect storms of opposition to arise. Expect negative thoughts to battle you. Expect other people to oppose you. Expect the enemy in any and every way to try to make you believe that you cannot be and do all that God has called you to be and do.

Do you imagine that the disciples had no opposing thoughts, as you do? Do you think they were so superpowerful that they never experienced difficulty in believing in what they were supposed to be and do and where they were to go? No, we have their stories, and we know their struggles. We see their failures. We even know what they thought on some occasions. On this particular occasion, they thought they were perishing, and their ministries had not even begun yet.

This Was God's Team

This was God's team. Some of these men would write sacred books of the Bible. These men would turn the world upside down. They would be the first to lay hands on the sick and see them recover, lay hands on the blind and see their eyes opened, speak to the lame and see them walk. But right at this moment all they could think about was how terrible that storm was and that their lives were about to be snuffed out.

Thank God Jesus was right there. He was with them. He was looking out for them. He was protecting them, keeping them safe from all harm — weather related or otherwise. Nothing was too hard for Him.

Jesus Was Disappointed in Them

Jesus was disappointed in them:

And he said unto them, Where is your faith?
Luke 8:25

In other words, Jesus was saying, "Why did you let this storm bother you? Why were you so sure you were perishing? Where is your faith?"

Today, Jesus still walks among us and calls us to His side. What has He called you to do? Does it look too big for you? If so, He asks you today, "Where is your faith?" Do you believe you can do whatever God speaks to you to do? If not, let Him increase your faith.

We all sometimes experience a lack of faith. After all, we know ourselves all too well and know that we are nothing. But just remember: He is everything. He can do it, and He will work through you to do it.

God gives us many things to do that we didn't ask for, didn't pray for, and didn't want. But He knows best and says to us, "This is good for you. It will bring you into a new place with Me. I am inviting you to come and go with Me to the other side, for I have some new horizons for you, some new places for you to go. I want you to do something you have never done before. In order to do it, you cannot look back to the things you've already accomplished. This is very different. Step out by faith and come with Me. We're going to the other side, and this will be, for you, a new beginning."

CALLED TO A NEW BEGINNING

Is God calling you to a new beginning? It might be a new book. It might just be a new chapter. It might be feeding those who are hungry. It might be going to the nations. It might be your first time to prophesy, or it might be your first time to lay hands on the sick and see them healed. It doesn't matter what it is that God is calling you to. What matters is that you get in the boat and go with Him.

Getting Out of the Boat

Then, when you have reached the other side, you have to get out, or nothing can be accomplished. There is a getting in, there's a going forth, and there's a getting out on the other side. And it's all important.

You might say, "But I don't know anyone there." That's okay. He does.

You might say, "But I don't know how to function in this strange place." That's okay, He does.

You might say, "I don't know what to say to these people." That's okay. He does. Just give yourself over to Him, and He will do the work. Let Him fill you, let Him carry you forth, and let Him cause you to be able *"to work the works of God"* (John 6:28). Jesus promised:

> *Verily, verily, I say unto you, He that believeth on me, the works that I do shall he do also; and greater works than these shall he do; because I go unto my Father.*
>
> John 14:12

Despite the storm that threatened all their lives, Jesus and the disciples got to the other side that day, and you can get there too.

Confronted by Something Very Unpleasant

Now, having miraculously reached the other side, the disciples were confronted by something very unpleasant.

The very first person they encountered in this new place was a man who was obviously full of demons and out of his right mind. He had been like this for a very long time, was living among the tombs, and didn't have a stitch of clothing on. We can only imagine what went through their minds right then.

When the man saw Jesus, he cried out, fell down at Jesus' feet, and began to say something very strange:

> *When he saw Jesus, he cried out, and fell down before him, and with a loud voice said, What have I to do with thee, Jesus, thou Son of God most high? I beseech thee, torment me not.* Luke 8:28

How odd! This man was obviously not in his right mind. He wore no clothes and could not live in the normal way, preferring to commune with the dead. But the moment he saw Jesus, he recognized Him as the Son of the Most High and fell down before Him.

The fact that the man spoke of Jesus tormenting him shows that it was not him speaking, but the demons in him speaking. Just the presence of Jesus was tormenting to those demons.

Not a Normal Case

Jesus now commanded the unclean spirit to come out of him, but this was not a normal case. The Scriptures tell us:

Oftentimes it had caught him: and he was kept bound with chains and in fetters; and he brake the bands, and was driven of the devil into the wilderness. Luke 8:29

This was a serious case. Jesus asked the man what his name was, and the answer came forth:

And he said, Legion: because many devils were entered into him. Luke 8:30

We all know the story:

And they besought him that he would not command them to go out into the deep. Luke 8:31

Jesus told the demons to go, and they came out immediately. They went into some swine that were feeding nearby, and the swine ran violently down the hill into the sea and were drowned. Wow! What an impact this must have made on the disciples. They had just witnessed a terrifying storm at sea and seen Jesus calm it with a few words. They had marveled at this and commented among themselves:

What manner of man is this! for he commandeth even the winds and water, and they obey him. Luke 8:25

Now they had seen a man who was severely demon possessed and, with just a few words, Jesus had set him completely free. Not only did Jesus control the winds and waves and have authority over them, but He also had power over all demons.

Not only did the demons obey Jesus and go out of the man, but he who had been so severely tormented was now totally normal and sitting at the feet of Jesus in his right mind.

Then they [the people of the town] *went out to see what was done; and came to Jesus, and found the man, out of whom the devils were departed, sitting at the feet of Jesus, clothed, and in his right mind: and they were afraid.*
Luke 8:35

Thank God for the fact that the man was in his right mind. He wants to put us in our right minds too.

If Jesus is calling us to the other side, we may not know what's over there, but we do know this: He will be with us, and He will set men and women free wherever we go.

Jesus Wasn't Condemning Them

Some make too much of the fact that Jesus asked the disciples where their faith was. He wasn't condemning them. He definitely did not say to them, "You'll never make it." He absolutely did not say to them, "I don't know why in the world I ever called you." He did not say to them, "How many times do I have to keep on telling you these things?"

"Where is your faith?" was enough. He was causing them to see that their faith had to be in Him, not in the weather or the boat they had boarded that day. If their faith was in Him, He could deliver them from any danger and set them free from any peril. And if your faith is in

Him, you can do great things too. Yes, you can even turn the world upside down. As the Scriptures say: *"Not by might, nor by power, but by my spirit, saith the Lord of hosts."*

It is He who has called you, He who will also fill you and equip you. He is entrusting *you* to carry His Word and to make His name known. This is not the time to be moving away from God. Some are actually getting out of the ministry, but God is calling us to get in.

You Must Get Out

Once you have reached the other side, don't insist on staying in the safety of the boat. Get out and face the world around you. Get out and tell men and women about Jesus. Get out of the boat. You have reached the other side, and this is the beginning of a whole new day for you. This new day will, no doubt, bring challenges and trials your way, but it will also bring you new joy, new strength, new ministry, new signs and wonders, and new and greater miracles in Jesus.

When I am called upon to face the daily challenges of the camp ministry (for instance, the huge light bills and propane gas bills, but also the spiritual challenges), I revert to one stance. I raise my hands high to Heaven and start taking steps forward. I know that I can't do it, but He can. He definitely can.

How I Thank God!

How I thank God for that first walk with Sister Edith Heflin, when she simply bowed her head and said, "Jesus,

You're so wonderful, and You never fail." I would like to leave that with you today: "Jesus, You're so wonderful, and You never fail." Make that your prayer as you go forth to do God's will for your life and ministry.

Amen!

CHAPTER 6

UNDERSTANDING THE SEED, PART II
BY PASTOR PETER KANGE

Do you still have that seed at hand? Take it in your hand. Look at it again. What great potential that seed holds. While you are reading this book, I want you to eat seed and sleep seed. I want seed to fill your mind and captivate your thoughts. Some of you need to do some fasting, as you seek God for His seed will for your life.

As I insisted in Chapter 3, many of you need to spend more time praying in the Spirit. Push aside some of the activities you had planned for the next few days and give time to seeking the face of God in the Spirit. This is your life we're talking about. This is your future that is at stake. Give God the time He needs to work on you.

UNDERSTANDING THE SEED

WHAT THE SCRIPTURES SAY

The Scriptures say of praying in the Holy Ghost:

But ye, beloved, building up yourselves on your most holy faith, praying in the Holy Ghost, keep yourselves in the love of God, looking for the mercy of our Lord Jesus Christ unto eternal life. Jude 1:20-21

For he that speaketh in an unknown tongue speaketh not unto men, but unto God: for no man understandeth him; howbeit in the spirit he speaketh mysteries.
1 Corinthians 14:2

He that speaketh in an unknown tongue edifieth himself. 1 Corinthians 14:4

I thank my God, I speak with tongues more than ye all.
1 Corinthians 14:18

Do it more and more, not less and less.

Praying in the Holy Ghost raises your spirit man to a place where you become more sensitive to God, so that you can hear Him better. So no child of God should have to be coaxed to pray in the Holy Ghost. Some believe that this type of prayer is very outdated, but they are so wrong. Nothing could be more modern and more important to our everyday life in the twenty-first century.

We didn't get to where we are today because of education, and the anointing of God is never purchased

Understanding the Seed, Part II

with money. No, the power we need comes only with seeking God.

Are you ready for change? Are you ready to become a seed in God's hands? Then seek Him for it.

We all need more prayer. Before you continue reading, please take some time now and pray in the Holy Ghost. Pray as you have never prayed before. Your vision depends on it. Your ministry depends on it. Hearing from God depends on it.

Let your spirit man ascend right now ... until you can break through, break loose, and break forth. Your most holy faith depends upon it.

I like what the Apostle Paul said:

My little children, of whom I travail in birth again until Christ be formed in you ... Galatians 4:19

Make your prayer a season of travail, and dare to take your prayer life to the next level. You will be richly rewarded.

Isaiah spoke of this great blessing of praying in the Holy Ghost:

For with stammering lips and another tongue will he speak to this people. Isaiah 28:11

As you pray in the Spirit, God's voice will become clearer to you. When you have finished, continue reading concerning the seed.

Understanding the Seed

Take Heed What You Hear

Now, let's continue with Mark 4. The Word of God says:

And he said unto them, Take heed what ye hear: with what measure ye mete, it shall be measured to you.
Mark 4:24

This is the Lord speaking to the seed. And who is the seed again? You and I are the seeds in this teaching.

"Take heed what ye hear." We must be careful what we listen to. To the degree we listen to God and His Word, to that same degree it will bear fruit in us. We will become the Word that we listen to.

This is very good news. It means that we can determine what we will become by choosing what we listen to.

Jesus went on to say in that verse:

And unto you that hear shall more be given.

Wow! How lovely! If we keep on listening, more will be given to us. This lets us know why the enemy works so hard to keep us from hearing more. He doesn't want us to have more. This is the reason we must know how to wage warfare against the things that attempt to divert us. It could be a person or a thing, or it could be Satan himself. His plan for us is not good, so he must be defeated.

Some of our friends think we go to church too much. "If you didn't go today, would the world come to an end?" they ask. My, isn't the enemy clever? He phrases things so nicely. What he neglects to say is that the more we listen to the seed, the more seed will be given to us.

We could also state this truth conversely or inversely, if you like: the less I listen, the less I will be given. It's just that simple. I need to listen, and so do you.

Your Portion Is Determined by What You're Listening To

The Word of God continues:

For he that hath, to him shall be given: and he that hath not, from him shall be taken even that which he hath.
Mark 4:25

What you have is considered your portion, based on what you are listening to. If you are no longer listening, meaning you have failed to continue to listen, the portion that was yours will cease to be yours. In order for it to always be yours, you must hear it and keep hearing it.

This is the secret of how to keep your healing. This is how to keep your deliverance. This is how to keep your ministry. You have to constantly hear about the seed.

What causes a couple to move from that wonderful honeymoon stage to the I-don't-want-to-see-your-face stage? During the honeymoon, it is: "You're the only thing I want to see," but then one or both keep hearing other suggestions. There is the you-have-so-many-discrepancies stage, and the I-never-knew-you-were-like-this stage. What we don't realize in that moment is that we're listening to the wrong things, and the more we listen to the wrong things, the more what we thought we had is being taken away from us. Why? Because of what we have listened to.

Again this shows that you can pretty much determine what you will have in life. What you want to have will become yours — if you keep listening to the right things.

If you want healing, keep listening to healing. When you have gotten past healing and are concerned with maintaining your health, listen to seeds that declare good health. Move from the I-need-to-be-healed stage to the I-am-determined-to-keep-my-good-health stage.

TV Is a Powerful Influence in the 21st Century

I fully understand everything that pops up on our TV these days about weight loss, and you can listen to it if you want. But allow me to give you some free advice. In order to get you to buy a product, I need to sell you an idea — the idea that you are not doing nearly as well as you thought you were doing. If that idea sounds true to you, and you continue to listen to it, you quickly become convinced that what you are hearing is the secret to your future wellbeing. With the use of that particular product, you could be in really great shape.

The end result is that you buy the product and thus negate the power of God that is in you to meet your every need. As you use that product, you become dependent upon it, and your health actually declines as a result. Do you see how subtly the enemy has spoken to you and convinced you to do his bidding?

EVE THOUGHT SHE WAS BEING EDUCATED

Eve didn't recognize who was talking to her in the garden. She thought she was being educated about fruit. And that's the same lie Satan is using today. We don't consider that we are being lied to. No, we are being "educated." We are becoming "knowledgeable" on a certain subject.

Most dieting goes contrary to the Word of God that declares:

> *For every creature of God is good, and nothing to be refused, if it be received with thanksgiving.*
>
> 1 Timothy 4:4

One day my wife and I and some of our members were on our way driving to the camp in Ashland, Virginia. We had left so late that the others agreed we could not possibly make it in time for the service. I chose to disagree. "We'll make it," I said.

"But look at the time," someone replied.

I answered, "I know, but I'm driving, so we'll get there when we need to get there."

There was traffic, of course, and it was a two-hour-and-thirty-minute drive, but I felt confident. The story has a good ending. We got to camp on time. Choose what you want to listen to, and depending on what you choose, life results will be measured to you.

It Is Measured Back To Us

God knows how to create things depending on the word we are listening to and believing in. It is measured back to us. The system is in place, and nothing can change it. The moment you start to listen, what you are listening to is measured back to you.

"Oh, poor me, poor me, poor me!" This thought will be measured back to you. "I came from such a poor family." This thought is even now being measured back to you.

Every Bible character who was thinking and/or speaking something contrary to the Word of God had to change what they were thinking and speaking in order to receive from Him. Until then, God's hands were tied. What we listen to determines what we think and/or speak, so take heed.

Abram Became Abraham

Abram had to change so dramatically that even his name was changed. One day he looked at Sarah, mother of many, and at himself, father of many, and realized that they were still childless. So he had to do something about that. In order for us to produce we have to start thinking and saying what it is we are determined to produce.

We saw that in Chapter 3. God spoke to the seed and said, "Bring forth after your kind," and the seed obeyed fully. Then, He turned to the work of man and said, "Let us make man after our image." In the greatest sense of the word, we are actually gods. We're not a bunch of wimpy people who can be tossed to and fro. Oh, beloved, take heed what you hear, because that's what will be measured back to you.

The Trials of 2010

In 2010, I had an unusual experience. Many saints were going through great trials that year. Our church split into many pieces, and when I would go to church and see less and less attending, I wondered to myself, "What in the world is going on?" Then a group of intercessors sent word to me, though not directly, that the church would close down totally by October of that year. This was not what I was hearing from God, so I decided to put a stop to this evil word immediately. I got in my car and started driving. I was on an extended retreat.

I drove south through Maryland, continued down through Virginia, on through North Carolina and also South Carolina. Only when I got to Atlanta, Georgia, did I feel led to stop and find a hotel.

I need to say here that I was not alone. I had taken another faithful brother and two faithful church sisters with me. There in Atlanta, we sought the face of God for a few days.

"When You Make Up Your Mind"

The first thing the Lord said to me was this: "When you make up your mind to come to the front, I will take you forward."

I said, "What?" I was perplexed, thinking that this is what I was doing all along. But I knew that this word was from God, and it got to me.

"Okay," I said. "Okay. Okay."

Then He told me something else. "Nobody asks directions from someone who looks confused."

I said, "What? Does that mean I look confused?" Oh, let me tell you, I had to face some very serious issues about myself in those days.

God said, "In ministry, you must know how to set priorities straight. For instance, ministry is not about people being slain. In case you have a ministry list with numbered items on it, and #5 on the list is people being slain, strike it out. Just strike it out."

So now I knew that I looked confused and I had my priorities wrong, and I needed to deal with these issues.

Next God told me, "When you make up your mind, I will show you that you've made up your mind."

"Do You Know Why?"

I decided to visit the church of Pastor Creflo Dollar. When I went in, some ushers hurried to help me find a place to sit. God said to me, "Do you know why they came to you? Because everything about you looked confused." Maybe you can identify with that. My mouth was closed, but my body language was speaking loudly.

The next day I went back again, and this time I walked purposely down the aisle as if I knew exactly where I was supposed to be sitting. Everyone around me greeted me warmly. No sooner had I sat down than the Lord said, "That's what I'm talking about."

I said, "Okay. That's fine. I got You."

Eventually I told Him, "I've made up my mind." I had sat in the back that day, and a lady now came to me. I still remember what she looked like. She said, "Sir, would you follow me?"

I followed her, and she took me all the way up to the front.

Now God said, "I like that, but you've not yet made up your mind to fight the odds. You've not yet made up your mind to go against the challenges. You have thought they were normal, so you stayed where you were. The day you will resolve that all of these challenges are not part of your life, then you will no longer want to be associated with them."

I had to see that these obstacles were just like speed bumps. You have a determined direction, and you must go where you are destined to go. Stop lingering with the bumps or talking about how they feel or how things are going. That's all mere conversation. Instead of wondering, "Who can deliver me?" you must understand that your actions determine your end.

When I got back from that retreat, what I had experienced changed everything for a ministry that people had declared would close down. That year, 2010, things began to turn around for us.

In 2011, the Lord said to me, "Make this place home." We were worshiping in a basement, but because God said to make it home, we set about to do just that. We got some paint and began to fix the place up.

Some of my members asked, "Why are we fixing *this* place up? Isn't that a waste of money?"

I said, "Because the Lord said so. All of this money we are 'wasting,' is no waste — if the Lord says to do it." We finished our renovations, and the place looked beautiful.

In 2012, the Lord said, "You've been faithful, and now I am taking you out." He did, and our journey has been interesting ever since. You have to know what you are listening to.

The Money Issues

During that retreat God also said to me, "Do you remember the person who owes you money?"

"Yes," I replied.

"Well, make it an offering to Me," He said.

I said, "What? What? What?"

I'm not talking about $500. I'm talking about $12,000.

"There are two things that can happen," the Lord said. "If you don't give it to Me as an offering, you will lose it because they won't give it, as they promised."

I called my wife, Pastor Pauline, hoping that she would say this idea was not from the Lord. Sometimes believers use a search for confirmation as an excuse to escape from an instruction they have clearly received. The more we talked, the more I knew it meant that we were doing the right thing. So I released the entire amount to the Lord. My heart bled for the $12,000, but I released it nonetheless. "My heart has bled for something less than twelve thousand dollars, and now I give it to You as an offering," I told the Lord.

He said, "That's good."

"Now, He continued, "Do you remember the $3,000 you received?"

"Yes," I said.

"Give it as another offering."

I said, "Okay. Okay. Okay. I will give it. I will give it." And I did.

Then He spoke to me about a third amount. He wanted that as an offering too. And I gave that amount too.

And what was the result of all of this? Recently I can't think of anything I have wanted to buy and was unable to do so. In the process of all of this, I have learned how to acquire the most expensive things. They are not purchased with money. They are purchased with God's favor.

Sometimes, when I have needed something, I went into a shop that sold it, laid my hands on it, and spoke to it. I said, "You know you need to come with me tomorrow." And God has done it for me. It has happened more than once.

"Send Some Offerings Back to Camp"

One day, when I was speaking with Pastor Jane Lowder about the many bills the Ashland Campground faces every month, she said to me, "This is my position before God," and she raised her hands to Him. When she did that, God spoke to me to send some offerings back to the camp after we had gotten back home, and we were blessed to do it. We began to experience in our ministry some of the same miracles that took place in the campground. Everything at camp is accomplished by faith, and sowing into that fertile ground has caused a release of similar miracles to us.

Of course, there were those who told me not to do it. It always happens. But thank God I was obedient. The more negative voices we hear, the more we need to press in to obey God in what He has told us to do. He will never discourage you from doing good, so if there is a discouraging voice, you can know for sure where it is coming from.

A Construction Project

A few months ago, we began a huge construction project. One day the Lord said to me, "You see this other part of the construction? That's your job."

I said, "My job?"

He said, "Yes, that is what you are going to do. This is not something the church will be involved in. This is your personal work of faith."

I said, "Really?"

He said, "Yes."

Not long before that, a minister had visited the church and encouraged the members to put in a special offering for their pastors. Once everything came in, it was between five and six thousand dollars. That was a great love gift.

Then one day my wife and I were discussing some gifts we wanted to buy for our members, When I reminded her of that offering, the Lord began to speak to me: "That money ... ," He said, "take it and start that work I talked to you about."

In the next service I made an announcement to the whole church: "I am starting a faith walk with God. I don't want the rest of you to feel guilty about it. This is my faith walk with the Lord."

Construction was starting, and the initial estimate of the cost was more than $24,000. But let me tell you that in 2013, for the first time since its founding, Reaching The Nations Ministries International in Maryland started supporting their pastors full-time.

A Special Miracle

This was a special miracle, and I'll tell you why. When we started the ministry in Beltsville, Maryland, one of the thing we decided, as pastors, was to remain completely disassociated from the finances. I recommend this practice to other pastors. If we can learn to manage the church in this way, it will make things flow with peace. God didn't call us to collect offerings; He called us to minister to people. If they decide to give offerings, that's fine.

We began the construction with an initial $5,000 worth of materials (from the love offering we had received, as mentioned earlier). The next day, the man in charge of the work crew called to say that he would not be able to start that day. It was taking him longer than anticipated to get his team together. He asked if it was okay with us for them to start on Tuesday.

I said, "Sure."

He asked, "Are the finances in place?"

I said, "Yes, just come by to get the money." (You need to learn how to answer in faith, too.)

The man came on Tuesday. I had gone to the bank just for the sake of going, and I was surprised to find that the account had about $12,000 that we had not been aware of. So the faith walk was on.

By the time the construction had been completed, the cost of the project had risen to nearly $50,000, and God had supplied it all. You may be wondering how you will do what God has planted in your heart to do. The answer is: He will do it. That's what seeds do; they reproduce after their kind.

Our Hearing Determines Our Harvest

Our hearing determines our harvest because our hearing produces a ertain culture. I love the way Hebrews 6 says it:

> *For God is not unrighteous to forget your work and labour of love, which ye have shewed toward his name, in that ye have ministered to the saints, and do minister.*
> Hebrews 6:10

We *"do minister."* We'll see a connection with this later. What God is talking to us about is not just something we have done in the past, but something we are still doing right now and will do in the future.

The text goes on to say:

> *And we desire that every one of you do shew the same diligence, to the full assurance of hope unto the end: that*

ye be not slothful, but followers of them who through faith and patience inherit the promises. Hebrews 6:11-12

So you keep on doing and doing, and that is the culture that is developed. As we saw in Chapter 3, based on Isaiah 55, this diligence produces a way of doing things. And when you are in a way of doing things, you then produce your harvest.

The Bible says that we must patiently and diligently do this. It's not, "Oh, how nice," and that's it. This is a continual effort. The day you decide that you will no longer continue, you stop the flow. You end the culture, and you begin to lose everything you have worked for until that moment. We don't want that, right?

These are key things that we must understand when it comes to being a seed. There is our hearing, and there is our speaking.

A Tree Is Known By Its Seed

Now let's look at Matthew's Gospel:

Either make the tree good, and his fruit good; or else make the tree corrupt, and his fruit corrupt: for the tree is known by his fruit. Matthew 12:33

How interesting, right? How do you produce the tree in the first place? From a seed.

Here we are told that a tree is known by it fruit, but there is another side to it. Whatever tree you are expecting, you must plant that particular seed. So a tree is not only known by its fruit; it is also known by its seed. This means that you can pretty much determine your harvest, based on what you plant.

We Learned about Seeds as Children

As we were growing up, Dad did some farming. I remember us pacing off land to plant. At a certain point, he would push a peg into the ground, making a little hole, and there a seed was to be planted. Then, if he did not reap the harvest he expected, we knew that the next year we had to add more land under cultivation and plant more seeds.

Long before a single seed went into the ground, Dad had to figure out more or less the size of the harvest he expected because he had to prepare some place to keep it. Only then did he go out and purchase enough seed to bring in that amount of harvest.

Once the seed was in hand, we walked carefully through the rows, placing the seed strategically in the holds he had made for them. "Don't just put one seed in each hill," he told us. "Put two seeds in each spot, and don't miss any spots." There was nothing dangerous about us missing a spot. Dad was thinking of the needed harvest, and that is our key, too. When your concentration is on the needed harvest, you will know what you must do to facilitate that harvest.

What does the Bible say? *"A man that hath friends must shew himself friendly"* (Proverbs 18:24). You must sow in order to reap.

In Matthew 12:35, Jesus said this:

Understanding the Seed, Part II

A good man out of the good treasure of the heart bringeth forth good things: and an evil man out of the evil treasure bringeth forth evil things.

Why is this true? Because, as He said in verse 34, *"For out of the abundance of the heart the mouth speaketh."* What does this mean? It means that when I am thinking of a treasure I want to produce, I have to begin to state what that treasure is, in order to be able to produce it. I have to primarily place that treasure into my heart, and the only way I can do that is by hearing about the treasure.

As I listen to the message about the treasure, I am hiding that treasure in my heart. Then I open my mouth, and I begin to talk about the treasure. That's me sowing seed. And the result will be that it is measured unto me.

Good Seed Produces Good Fruit

Your children can become obedient children. You just need to put the right thing into your heart. Someone might say, "Are you saying that I haven't done everything I should do as a parent?" Well, let's put it this way: Why not forget what you have done in the past and start over, and this time do things differently.

Your business can change. Your finances can change. You can have that TV you've been wanting, and you won't have to pay for it.

Now, please don't try to walk out of a store with a TV set you haven't paid for and tell them I gave you permission to do so. Some people take God's Word and try to make it say what they want.

What am I trying to say here? Put the right things into your heart, speak the right words, and you will produce what you need to produce.

"Lift Up Thine Eyes"

It fascinates me to read about God speaking to Abraham and saying:

> *Lift up now thine eyes, and look from the place where thou art northward, and southward, and eastward, and westward: for all the land which thou seest, to thee will I give it, and to thy seed for ever. And I will make thy seed as the dust of the earth: so that if a man can number the dust of the earth, then shall thy seed also be numbered. Arise, walk through the land in the length of it and in the breadth of it; for I will give it unto thee.*
>
> Genesis 13:14-17

It was all to be given to Abraham, but what was the first thing he had to do to get it? He had to go out and *see* the land he wanted God to give him. When he obeyed and went out and surveyed the land, what he saw entered his heart, and God gave it to him. That's how it works.

"The Lord Said in His Heart"

Genesis 8:21 says the following:

Understanding the Seed, Part II

And the LORD smelled a sweet savour; and the LORD said in his heart, I will not again curse the ground any more for man's sake; for the imagination of man's heart is evil from his youth; neither will I again smite any more every thing living, as I have done.

Did you notice that God said something *"in his heart"*? Why? Because when He smelled the *"sweet savour,"* it got into his heart. It spoke something to Him, and so He began to speak, and He *"said in his heart ... ."* He said that He would never again curse the ground for man's sake. Where did the inspiration for this thought come from? It came from one man whose heart was right toward God. That man was Noah.

Where and When Did This System Begin?

It was then that God declared:

While the earth remaineth, seedtime and harvest, and cold and heat, and summer and winter, and day and night shall not cease.   Genesis 8:22

We know very well that this system did not begin at that moment or in that place. It began all the way back in Genesis 1 or, in other words, in the beginning, and it continued in force from that time.

Our Dominion

God spoke to Noah:

Understanding the Seed

Bring forth with thee every living thing that is with thee, of all flesh, both of fowl, and of cattle, and of every creeping thing that creepeth upon the earth; that they may breed abundantly in the earth, and be fruitful, and multiply upon the earth.   Genesis 8:17

Noah was not to fear any of the animals because he was their master. They would fear him.

One day, as I was walking down a road, the Lord said to me, "There's a snake."

I said, "Oh, yes, a snake."

"What do you want to do with it?" He asked.

"Nothing," I said. I went my way, and the snake went his way.

God's people are destined in such a way that even if they eat and/or drink deadly things, they will not be hurt. If they pick up ravenous beasts, they will suffer no harm. There is a wonderful example of this in the Bible.

Paul was shipwrecked on an island called Melita. The local people warmly received the distressed passengers and built a fire to help them dry off. As Paul was putting some sticks into the fire, a snake came out and bit him, fastening itself onto his arm. The local people, seeing what had happened, supposed that he must be an evil man who was now receiving his just reward, and they expected him to fall dead any minute. When, instead, he showed no fear and simply shook the serpent off into the fire, they marveled and decided that he must be a god. He knew that he had dominion, so he was not frightened by the serpent.

Understanding the Seed, Part II
Things Can Get Better

God is saying to us that things can get better ... if we intently desire it to be so. But these things must be approached with intention. You have to say, "This is how I want things to become." Then go ahead and fill yourself with the substance that will produce the thing you are intently desiring. Begin to talk about it, even if you don't feel anything.

Some have said, "Fake it until you make it," but, to me, that's not what we're talking about. I think, when they say, "Fake it," it's only because people understand the concept better in those terms. But there is nothing fake about this approach.

When you speak something out in faith, you are definitely not faking it. Saying it with intent and saying it with passion (declaring it, if you will) shows that it is coming from your heart because you have filled your heart with it. That kind of determined faith will be rewarded. That seed definitely *will* bear fruit.

We ministers spend time in the Word of God, and our purpose is not just to find sermon material. We, too, need to be fed. We, too, need divine seeds to be planted in our hearts. There is seedtime, and there is harvest, and the one cannot come without the other.

Isaac's Case

God told Isaac not to leave Gerar, even though there was a famine in the land. Isaac obeyed that word, and he became that word. He so believed God that he dared to do what no one else was doing. He sowed in the land of famine, and the results were stunning:

> *Then Isaac sowed in that land, and received in the same year an hundredfold: and the L<small>ORD</small> blessed him.*
>
> Genesis 26:12

When did he receive it? *"In the same year."*

Why did this happen? Because Isaac took to heart the word God spoke to him, hid it in his heart, believed it, and then acted upon it. And this system will work for you, too. Your time of famine can be turned into blessing.

What Is Success?

Success is difficult to measure in ministry. It is certainly not about big buildings. Scratch that one off of your success list. Churches that are all about growing people's lives are successful, no matter how large or small. But this may not be what people want to hear these days. They would much rather hear about step-by-step techniques on how to receive the answers they want. Using a certain strategy, you are told, will attract people to your church, and that may sound good to many, but it is not a viable plan.

The plan we need is how to be more longsuffering with people until they can grow up and become mature men and women of God. This has nothing to do with how many cars you have in your garage. If one of your cars has an accident and is out of service, does that mean you are suddenly no longer successful?

Success in the ministry has nothing to do with how much or how little you are appreciated or praised. It has nothing to do with how many awards you have received. Success is much more than that.

The Appearance of Success

Some people seem to be very successful in business, and yet when their children fail to do well in school, they sink into despair. Success, for them, is not about the money they are earning. It's about the welfare of the children they love.

We must all define success for ourselves, setting the goals that are meaningful to us personally. Some ministers have great churches, but they are some of the saddest people on earth because that is not what fulfills them personally. The Word of God can help us to bring the proper balance to everything we do.

What the Word *Success* Really Means

When I looked up the word *success* I was amazed at what I found. English is a language that borrows from many other languages, and often we must go back and look at the origin of the word in that other language or languages to see exactly what it means today. Originally *success* meant "coming close to" or "making it after all." When we can say, "Despite everything that came against me, I made it," that's success. That's being successful. That's succeeding.

There is another important element to success. We must not only be able to say, "I made it after all." We must also be able to say, "I didn't stop making it. I am still making it." Success, therefore, is not just something we have had in the past; it refers to what we are doing right now.

There is one more element to the word. It not only means that I have made it in the past and am currently making it. It infers the all-important question: "so what are you going to do next?" Success does not mean that you have arrived. It simply points to the next step.

Let's Take It a Step Further

Since we are talking about seeds, and this book is entirely directed to seeds, let's take this a step further: When a seed is put into the ground, its dies, and then small blades come out and push their way through the soil to the waiting sunshine. But growth does not end there. The plant keeps on growing. Even when the plant has reached full maturity, growth does not end. It just changes. So there is one step, then another step, then another step, then another step, then another step, then another step, and then another step. But none of those steps is necessarily easy.

Think a moment, for example, of that seed under the soil. Soil is under it, soil is over it, and soil is all around it. As it attempts to grow, the soil presses in on it from every direction. What can a tiny seed do under such difficult circumstances? How can it possibly overcome all of this resistance? A key can be found in the Proverbs:

> *Drink waters out of thine own cistern, and running waters out of thine own well.* Proverbs 5:15

What does this have to do with seeds? Well, a seed cannot call for help from any other quarter. The rocks and dirt will not come to its rescue. It must rely on the strength it has within. It is a seed, and a seed has power within it to overcome all obstacles. Seeds come up through tiny cracks in concrete. Plants even break and push concrete out of their way.

All of the elements seem to be conspiring against that seed, determined that it will not come up and produce. But despite all of that, the seed not only survives; it thrives. And the resulting plant is amazing to behold.

Nothing can prevent a seed from coming up, and the reason is that it relies on the strength stored within it. You, as a good seed, need to be praying more in the Holy Ghost, building up your inner strength, so that you can overcome everything that opposes you in life.

A seed must give birth to a new plant, and that plant must grow. Why? Because that's what a seed does. A seed is not meant to be kept in the barn. It is meant to be planted so that it can produce. And when it has been planted, nothing can prevent it from producing. When a seed is in the ground, it has been given everything it needs to grow and prosper. Now, it's up to the seed.

UNDERSTANDING THE SEED

IT DOESN'T REALLY MATTER WHAT THE SOIL WANTS

So, as good seed, we must be praying in the Holy Ghost, and we must be taking in the Word of God. When this is done faithfully, it doesn't really matter what the soil wants. It cannot resist us. We *will* grow, and we *will* produce a harvest.

When Isaac sowed his seed, the circumstances were not good. No one else was wasting seed on such parched ground. They were in a famine. It was not raining as it should. But I hear God saying something to His people, His seeds. He is saying:

> *Arise, shine; for thy light is come, and the glory of the* LORD *is risen upon thee.*   Isaiah 60:1

What is God saying? He is saying: "You are good seed. You have strength within. Break loose from everything that oppresses you. Come forth from all that opposes you. 'Rise, shine.'"

At first, we may not see that anything at all is happening, but underneath the ground a miracle is taking place. A tiny root has shot forth and is making its way downward, seeking moisture. That root is tender and delicate, but it pushes on into the darkness ever deeper, determined to find a source of life.

How can this plant endure so much? The Scriptures give us a key:

Understanding the Seed, Part II

Looking unto Jesus the author and finisher of our faith; who for the joy that was set before him endured the cross, despising the shame, and is set down at the right hand of the throne of God. Hebrews 12:2

It was joy that enabled Jesus to endure the cross, and it is the joy of the Lord working in us that will empower us to withstand anything that comes our way and to come out victorious. Others might say, "You can't make it," but they're wrong. We are a seed, and a seed has potential that cannot be easily snuffed out.

We Can Endure

When something happens, and pain comes to us, we can endure that pain because we are a seed, and seeds have potential in them to survive anything that may try to hinder them.

Success, at this moment, does not depend on anything I did yesterday or last year. It depends on my next step. This was the reason Paul declared:

Yea doubtless, and I count all things but loss for the excellency of the knowledge of Christ Jesus my Lord: for whom I have suffered the loss of all things, and do count them but dung, that I may win Christ. Philippians 3:8

God wants our eyes to be focused on what is coming, not on what has been in the past. Where you are going right now is the important thing. If someone comments, "You won't make it," just ignore them and ask God, "What is my next step?"

Focus on Your Next Step

Success is not the next big house; it's your next step. And you can make it.

Someone might say, "You know that you're from a very poor family." Who cares? What difference does it make? If someone else has a problem with that, then that's their problem, not yours. Don't focus on the fact that your family has no money. Focus on your next step.

You only need to take one step at a time. If someone says, "This thing is so very difficult, no one has ever really done it successfully," just ignore them and look for your next step. You can make it.

If you can see your way to make one step, that's enough for now. Take that one step, and the way to the next one will become clearer. It doesn't matter that situations and people seem to be coming against you. Just look for that next step. That next step means success, and you can make it.

So that's what success is — my next step. If I can make it, then I will know that I am succeeding.

Success, for some, is being able to forgive someone for a past offense. For others, success is being able to tithe on a consistent basis. Whatever your next step is, declare to the devil: "You cannot stop me. I am the seed of God, and He has built strength into me. Nothing can keep me from success."

Understanding the Seed, Part II

Rest in the promises of God which say that you are the righteousness of God in Christ Jesus (see 2 Corinthians 5:21). Remind the devil of it.

Someone may have told you, "You can't preach. You haven't had enough schooling." Trust God. You are His seed, and He has placed strength in you. Open your mouth, and release His message. Lay your hands on the sick, and they will recover. Take that next step.

That Seed Represents You

Do you still have your seed handy? Hold it in your hand again. That seed represents you. Get ready to release it into the ground.

Talk to that seed. Remind it of its potential. Tell it what it can be in God. Speak success to that seed. Speak diligence to that seed. Speak increase to that seed. Tell it what it is about to do, what it is about to become. Tell it what an amazing life it has inside of it and that you are about to release it into the ground so that it can produce its destined fruit. As you are speaking out these truths, I trust that God is echoing them back to your soul. You are that seed.

Now, release the seed and stand back to watch what God will do.

Amen!

Chapter 7

Rebuilding a City
by Dr. Harold McDougal

The words of Nehemiah the son of Hachaliah.
It came to pass in the month of Chislev, in the twentieth year, as I was in Shushan the citadel, ² that Hanani one of my brethren came with men from Judah; and I asked them concerning the Jews who had escaped, who had survived the captivity, and concerning Jerusalem. ³ And they said to me, "The survivors who are left from the captivity in the province are there in great distress and reproach. The wall of Jerusalem is also broken down, and its gates are burned with fire."
⁴ So it was, when I heard these words, that I sat down and wept, and mourned for many days; I was fasting and praying before the God of heaven.
Nehemiah 1:1-4, NKJV

The King James Version the Bible calls this place *Susa* and says it was a *palace*. The use of the word *citadel* here, meaning a fortified palace, gives us a little better idea of just what a grand palace this was where Nehemiah was working.

A Casual Conversation Produces a Unique Burden

One day he was having a casual conversation with some travelers from his homeland. He asked about the holy city, and the answer he received was a sad one. No effort had been made to rebuild the city. Its walls were still broken down, and its gates were still in ashes. What was worse: as a result of the loss of protection, his people were living in great distress and reproach under the hand of their enemies round about.

Something happened when Nehemiah heard these words. He wasn't able to forget them, and they bothered him day and night. For some reason, he felt a burden for the downtrodden people of Jerusalem, and he couldn't rest until he did something about it.

We all know the story, and that helps me because I don't have to review all the details here. The crux of the story is that Nehemiah became the governor of Judah and ruled it for twelve years. This was a great miracle because when this burden came to him, he was a servant in the palace in Shushan. How would God send him back to his native land? How would a mere servant rally the people and rebuild the city of Jerusalem? It's a truly amazing story.

To me, this is one of the most wonderful stories in the Bible, and the details of it are powerful guides for us in many ways. Perhaps we are not called to rebuild a city, but we can use the same tactics Nehemiah used to do whatever God has called us to do.

Every Ministry Begins with a Burden

As we saw with Ananias in chapter 2, we can see here again that every ministry begins with a burden. It begins with a vision. It begins with some touch of God upon our lives. Suddenly and without warning, something touches us deep inside. We can't understand it, but it causes us to lose sleep and to have no normal appetite for food.

Nehemiah wept and prayed for many days, and he fasted. In fact, the rest of the chapter records some of the things he said to God in his prayers. It all began with a burden, and that burden drove Nehemiah to prayer.

A Burden Becomes a Call

In the process of seeking God, at some point this burden became more than a burden to Nehemiah; it became a call. This same thing happened to Paul when he had a dream and saw a man from Macedonia saying to him, *"Come over into Macedonia, and help us"* (Acts 16:9). When he woke up the next morning, he had a desire to go to Macedonia and find that man who needed his help. He'd had other plans. There had been other things on his mind, but that all changed now, and he was obsessed with this new desire.

Some of us have our future all mapped out, and suddenly our world is turned upside down because we have felt a burden from God. We don't understand it, but we can't shake it off. Every ministry must be birthed by feeling the heartbeat of God. Don't start something until you know what He wants.

Nehemiah Took His Burden to the Lord in Prayer

Nehemiah did the right thing. He took his burden to the Lord in prayer. Sometimes a burden is nothing more than a burden. We are to pray and intercede for someone in need, nothing more. This is a common experience among believers. If that's all it is, be faithful to your burden.

Don't jump and run to Macedonia every time you feel a burden. First, we must pray and find out what God means by what He is showing us. You have a sense that you need to do something. Is that something just to pray? If so, then be faithful in prayer.

The Burden Intensifies

Many times, however, it happens to us as it did to Nehemiah. When we have been faithful to pray, the burden does not lift. It only intensifies. And, while you are praying, it suddenly dawns on you what is happening: As you have been praying for someone to get a burden to return to Jerusalem, rally the people, and rebuild the city, you have been called to be that person you have been praying for. God has answered your prayer, and in the process, He has called you to do more than just pray. You are the man (or you are the woman).

Prayer is a good place to start, but when God is calling you to action, it goes far beyond prayer. It goes far beyond tears, far beyond fasting and prayer. You may be called to restore a people and rebuild a city. For some reason, this is always the most shocking discovery for us. God has given me the burden because I am the one He wants to do the work. During the days of Nehemiah's prayer and fasting, he came to the realization that he somehow needed to get back to Jerusalem. He somehow needed to rally these despondent people. And he somehow needed to rebuild the city.

Faithful to the First Steps

Perhaps, at the first, Nehemiah knew nothing about ultimately becoming governor and ruling over the people of Judah. That may have developed much later, as he was faithful to the first steps of his vision. We don't have to have the whole revelation in order to get started. Part of it is enough at first, and the rest will be revealed as we are faithful in the first steps.

If a vision seems too great for us, we might not be able to handle it. So sometimes the Lord gives it to us in little pieces so that we don't faint. Perhaps Nehemiah was planning a short trip back to Jerusalem, just long enough to get the work done. We don't know. God had a much longer-term mission in mind for him, but Nehemiah may not have known that at the time. Stay open to God, and every step will eventually be revealed.

My Sixty Days Become Seven Years

When I arrived in the Philippines in early 1967, my intention was to stay sixty days. That was what my visa allowed, and another brother was due there to take over the work. But God's plan was different. I was actually there for the next seven years. Sister Gwen Shaw was leaving Manila that day, and we crossed paths as we were leaving the airport and she was arriving. She asked us to come back and have a time of fellowship with her before her flight left for Hong Kong.

We all filed into the Happy Landing Lounge to have a glass of pineapple juice, and as we sat around the table about to drink our juice, someone asked her if she would pray. Her prayers were powerful, and when she prayed that day, she began to prophesy everything that would happen during the next seven years. I was thinking: "Wow! God is going to do all of that in sixty days! How amazing!" Of course, it wasn't sixty days but seven years.

Be open to God. Maybe your work will finish in sixty days (or six days), but maybe it will take twelve years. God is in charge, not you. Be prepared to do His will, and He will lead you one step at a time.

Nehemiah Was Not a Free Man

One of the most amazing things about this story is that Nehemiah was not free to make such a decision. He was one of the Judean captives who had been carried into exile, and he served at the king's pleasure. The land of Israel and Judah had been stripped of all riches, and the best of the young people, those who could excel in learning languages and the science of the day, had been carried away captive. Nehemiah was a slave in a foreign land.

There was, of course, a reason for all of this. The people had backslidden and were no longer serving God as they should. They needed some suffering to bring them back to Him. Everything in life has a reason. Now, however, God was about to redeem them and begin to restore their fortunes, and he chose Nehemiah to do it. But the man was not only living in a strange land among strange people; he was enslaved to them.

Because of this, Nehemiah was not free to make a decision and simply announce: "I've decided to go to Jerusalem to rebuild the city." And this was only the first of many impossibilities he had to face.

Why Would He Want to Go?

When you think about it, why would Nehemiah even want to go back to a city that was impoverished and left in ruins? He was living in the palace. This fact alone tells us that he was a man who had over time earned the people's respect. He had even earned the respect of the king. Because poison was a common form of assassination in those times, the king's cup bearer was always among the most trusted men in the kingdom. The fact that Nehemiah was a foreigner and still trusted by the king makes it all the more amazing. Why would he leave such a position?

But God saw the same things in Nehemiah that the king did and knew that Nehemiah would make a wonderful governor. God knew that Nehemiah could encourage those despondent people and rally them to work hard and rebuild their city, accomplishing a fete that we still marvel at today. So God called him anyway, despite the impossibilities.

The fact that Nehemiah was not free to go was now God's problem, and if God calls you and you're not free to obey Him, He'll make a way for you, too, miraculously removing every obstacle in your path. If there is a problem that you are powerless to do anything about, then it's not your problem. It's God's problem. He can do something about it, and He *will* do something about it.

ANOTHER PROBLEM AROSE

As Nehemiah prayed and considered what he should do, another problem arose. It was against the law to ever show sadness or other negative emotion in the presence of the king. If this law was not obeyed, it was a common practice for the king to call for the head of the person showing the negative emotion. Surely this was another reason Nehemiah had been chosen for this position in the first place. He was a cheerful person.

Now, however, Nehemiah was troubled. What he had heard about his people and his land was no laughing matter. He prayed and he fasted, for he was burdened.

Rebuilding a City

Suddenly he became terrified that he could not successfully conceal his concern from the king. By accepting this burden, he was placing his life in danger. At any moment the king could turn on him and have him executed.

Nehemiah was right to be concerned. The king quickly noticed the sadness. He had never before seen Nehemiah sad, so he couldn't help but see the contrast. His servant was sad, and he wanted to know why.

What should Nehemiah say at this moment? To suggest that after the king had elevated him and trusted him, he now wanted to leave and go somewhere else seemed unthinkable. To suggest that he wanted time off to make a journey back to his country didn't seem to make sense. But what could he say? The king had asked, so Nehemiah just blurted it all out.

"Your Highness, I have this great burden. I have learned that my people are living in a deplorable condition. The gates of our holy city have been burned, the walls are broken down, and our people live in abject poverty."

All of this should not have mattered to the king, since it was his own people who had caused all of this destruction to begin with, but he now surprised Nehemiah by asking, "What can I do to help?"

Nehemiah saw his opening and stopped to pray again. He didn't want to say the wrong thing, to spoil this amazing moment, to ask for himself and not for God's purposes. When he knew he had heard from Heaven, he became very bold. He was polite, but he now asked the king to send him to Jerusalem.

The king surprised him by answering, "When do you want to leave? And how long do you plan to be gone?" There is no logical explanation for this. When God calls us to do something, He works in amazing ways to make all the details come together. Leave it to Him to make a way, and He will.

Nehemiah Had Other Worries

Nehemiah had other worries. For example, how would he get through all the enemy territory between Shushan (in modern-day Iran) and Jerusalem? Travel in those days was extremely expensive and extremely dangerous. Nations were not committed to mutual treaties of respect for one another. To travel was to take your life into your own hands.

Nehemiah's boldness was rising. He now asked the king to send letters to important leaders along the way, telling them to let him pass safely. It must have amazed and thrilled him when the king not only agreed to the request for letters, but also offered to send a mounted guard to escort Nehemiah through every danger and be sure that he arrived at his destination safely. God knows how to do it all.

How Would Nehemiah Obtain Building Materials?

Another problem: How would Nehemiah obtain the materials he would need for the rebuilding? The people of Judah were living in poverty. Such materials were jealously guarded, and so they were terribly expensive — if they could be found at all. I can only imagine what Nehemiah felt when the king agreed to give him letters to those who controlled the forests so that they would provide the timbers needed for the rebuilding. Wow! God is so good.

As for stone, there was plenty of stone around Jerusalem. In some cases, they could reuse stones that had fallen from the wall. If they needed more, it was not hard to find.

Imagine it. Nehemiah hadn't even had time to develop his mailing list. He hadn't had time to inform his prayer partners about what he was feeling in his spirit, and already God was bringing it to pass, one step at a time. It is miracles like this that bring glory to God.

Nehemiah Got to Jerusalem

Nehemiah got to Jerusalem, and that was an important step. All of the things that happened on his journey are not even recorded, because they're not important. The important thing is that he got there. Who tried to impede him along the way and who was there to do what mischief is not important. Push it all aside and get there, and something wonderful will happen.

Today we rejoice when we see the walls of Jerusalem, and we love her gates. We love to go in and out of every one of them. We love to walk around on top of the walls and pray and claim God's promises. It's just a wonderful place, an anointed place of great history and spiritual significance. But the sight that greeted Nehemiah when he got there was very different. It must have been a shock to see the place so devastated.

For the first three days Nehemiah didn't do anything. What he was thinking and what he was feeling we can only guess. Then, on the third night, he took a donkey and went out to ride around the walls and do a little survey. Until that moment, he hadn't told a soul what his burden was, what was in his heart to do. And that was wise.

BE CAREFUL WHO YOU SHARE YOUR VISION WITH

Be careful who you share your vision with because most people will try to discourage you. They will not be able to understand what is in your heart. So share it with only a few. Call Lady Jane Lowder or other staff members of Calvary Campground. They will be happy for you, they will rejoice with you, and they will pray for the detail of your vision to come to pass. For the first three days, Nehemiah told no one.

There were recognized elders in Judah at the time. These men had risen to the top as leaders among the people, but they were very corrupt and were oppressing each other with heavy taxes for personal gain. Nehemiah didn't bother to tell these men anything about his burden. They might well have opposed him. He just mounted his donkey and rode around those fallen walls, praying and seeking guidance from God.

Tell me, what does a cup bearer know about rebuilding a city? How does such a man get a group of despondent, dejected, and depressed people to rise up and take the initiative to start rebuilding? How does he get them to work together to accomplish anything at all? How does he convince them that he can lead them any better than anyone else? How does he convince the people that he has a workable vision? No wonder he was out there riding around the walls praying. He didn't know what to do or how to do it.

Nehemiah needed prayer, and you and I do too. There are many important decisions to be made in the Kingdom of God, and they will affect more than one group of people or a single city. They will affect the future of nations and the future of great ministries that will touch those nations.

You cannot afford to make any old decision. You cannot afford to put just anyone in a position of trust and responsibility. You must make the right decisions, and then rest in your right decisions, and let God do the rest.

When someone is needed for a certain position, seek God for the right person for that position, and then put the person He indicates for that position, even if that person does not appear to have all of the necessary qualifications. Believe God to raise them up to meet the challenge.

Nehemiah Announces His Intentions

It appears that this one night of riding around the walls was enough for Nehemiah. The very next day he called the people together and began to share his vision. It was time, and he was ready. He told them:

You and I working together are going to rebuild this city. We will rebuild these fallen walls. We will make and install new gates. We will then rid the city of the heavy and unjust taxes that are oppressing you. We will overcome the enemies who have camped around you and for too long have taken advantage of you, robbing all that you have and taking it for themselves. Step by step, we will restore you to prosperity.

I don't know how tall or how short Nehemiah was. I don't know what his voice was like. I can't say how impressive a figure he was standing before them that day. Were they afraid of him because he was someone who had been living with a foreign king? Or did they perhaps despise him because of that very fact? All I know is that somehow he convinced them to hear his vision and follow him in the days ahead. And that is the gift of leadership. If no one is following you, then you're not a leader. Become a leader, and people will follow you.

The What, but Also the How of It

One of the important elements to Nehemiah's leadership was that he not only told the people what God said they should do; he told them how they were going to do it. Just as God had given a very precise and detailed plan to Moses on the mountain about how to build the wilderness tabernacle, God showed Nehemiah how to organize the people to rebuild Jerusalem.

Nehemiah now assigned a family to work together on each of the city gates, and he assigned other families to work together on certain portions of the walls. These people had been confused, depressed, and down, and they would have had no idea where to start, but he told each of them what they were to do. That takes great wisdom and shows us why God chose this particular man who had been hidden away in a palace serving the king. He'd had a nice life there, but he was willing to give it all up to go do the will of his God.

The way Nehemiah organized the workers makes me think of the Body of Christ. We are all members one of another, but we are organized in smaller families. Each congregation represents one of those families, and we each have our particular corner of the harvest field to reap.

It is not for us to say if the other families are doing their job well or not. Our concern is to get our part right. That is all that God requires of us. Do what God has called you to do, and let Him worry about the rest.

Some Enemies Get Nervous

What happened next? No sooner had the work begun than the enemies who lived all around the city got very nervous. At first, they only mocked and scorned. What Nehemiah was suggesting, they said, could never happen. Then, as the work picked up speed, they got increasingly upset about it and began to threaten.

You probably already know how upset the devil gets when you start doing something for God. If you haven't faced it yet, you surely will, so get ready.

Understanding the Seed

Next the enemies demanded that Nehemiah come down to talk things over with them. They had been ruling over Jerusalem for many years. He couldn't just come in and change things this way. Who did he think he was? I love Nehemiah's answer. "Tell them that we are too busy building. We cannot come down and argue with them. We have a job to do for God." What does that tell us? We should leave the opposition to God. He will take care of it. Just stay busy doing what you know to do, and you'll be fine.

Facing Armed Resistance

The next thing we know, these enemies were so enraged that they had risen up and were coming with their armies. Their intention was to forcibly remove the people and, thus, stop their work. Now, it was not just threats. These people were armed, and there were many of them.

If you have never felt threatened in your ministry, get ready. Those threats will surely come. When it was just threats, Nehemiah said, "We're too busy," but now they had to defend themselves or they would all die.

They prayed and came up with two ideas about defending themselves. One idea was to hold a tool in one hand and a weapon in the other. That seems like a very cumbersome way to work, and I can't imagine how they could have gotten much done. They settled on a second idea.

This idea was to work as normal, but they would each keep a sword close at hand and be ready to fight at a moment's notice. Each family would have a trumpet that they could blow if they came under attack. The order was that when any trumpet was heard, everyone would rush to the aid of the family under attack. One family could not hope to drive such a large group of enemies away, but if they all fought together, they could win.

I love this idea so much that I recommend it to everyone and propose that we adopt it as our official policy in the Kingdom of God. We're all in this together. If we would stop trying to fight our own battles (and stop fighting each other) and join forces to help each other, we could win every time.

If we all die then we all die together, but if we all live, we all live together. Let's vow to help each other. You work on your part of the wall, but if you need my help, blow the trumpet, and I'll come running. As you work, keep a sword strapped to your side, and be ready to fight at any moment. If you hear a trumpet sound, you'll know that I need your help. Please come running.

Wouldn't it be wonderful if we could implement such a plan today? Instead, when we hear our brothers blow the trumpet today and know that they are in trouble, we say, "I knew they were going to have trouble; you know how they are," and we go on our merry way. God is calling us to run to each other's rescue.

Clarence Ellis' Testimony

I loved the testimony of my Brother Clarence Ellis given in the ministers' conference. I hadn't heard it before.

He said he was lying at death's door, but his wife, Sister Phyllis, knew how to blow the trumpet, and Sister Jane Lowder heard that trumpet call and came to their rescue, helping them to overcome the enemy that threatened his very existence. It will work for you, too.

WITHOUT MY BROTHERS, I WOULD BE DEAD

There was a time when I, too, was at death's door. During all the years I had worked in the Philippines, I had never been seriously ill. We had all of the symptoms of various illnesses, but we prayed them away and went on. Some of our missionaries turned green with typhoid, and we prayed, and they were healed and went on.

Then I went back after being away for eight years, and after being there some weeks, suddenly came down with malaria, typhoid fever, and a serious kidney infection — all at the same time. I had to cancel all of my meetings, because I couldn't do a thing. I couldn't feed myself. I couldn't bathe myself. I was as helpless as a baby. My Filipino brothers took me to a hospital and never left my bedside for the next ten days.

When I experienced terrible chills, they would use their own bodies to warm me. When I was too weak to reach for a glass of water, they held it to my lips. It was a very humbling experience for a man of my age to have someone bathe me, but I had no choice. I simply could not do it for myself. How could I ever forget that experience? If it hadn't been for them, I would never have made it.

For ten days I was in a delirium, and horrid drug-inspired scenes flashed before my eyes, so that I felt like I was losing my mind. They stayed right there, all night and all day, every day, and they prayed. And on the tenth day, God raised me up. That all happened many years ago, back in the 1980s, and I've been able to do many things since then, but only because my brothers helped me. We need each other.

The Most Amazing Fact

I must conclude this chapter, and I want to conclude with this most amazing fact: in just fifty-two days (read it for yourself), the work of rebuilding the city of Jerusalem was completed. It happened because of a cup bearer, who knew nothing of engineering, architecture, carpentry, or masonry. In just fifty-two days, all of the walls were raised, and all of the gates were replaced. With all of our modern machinery, I don't think we could do that today. These days it takes fifty-two days or more just to get started. Maybe they didn't have to remake the foundations. Perhaps they were still intact, but to raise up those walls in fifty-two days was a marvelous feat. In just fifty-two days, the work was complete.

The enemies who had threatened them gathered in the valley below, and they were the depressed ones now. They had not been able to stop the work of God.

Read it all for yourself. It's a wonderful story. And the important thing is that God will do it for you, too.

Amen!

CHAPTER 8

THE ACTIVATION OF THE SEED
BY PROPHETESS ANDY McDOUGAL

We are experiencing a divine encounter in these days, and a definite shift has taken place in our lives. For my part, the things I have been declaring and prophesying during the past twelve to fourteen years are finally coming to fruition. And many of you, I trust, are stepping into the day, the hour, and the moment that I call *"the fullness of time."*

I want to speak to you prophetically in this chapter, I want to include many things, and I believe the Lord will help me to get every bit of it in.

THE REVELATION OF HIDDEN TRUTHS

I like to start many of my meetings by using Mark 4. The reason I love it is that the disciples asked Jesus about the parables He was teaching:

> *And as soon as He was alone, those who were around Him, with the Twelve [apostles], began to ask Him about the parables.* Mark 4:10, AMP

Understanding the Seed

This seemed, to the disciples, to be a strange way to teach. Why was Jesus apparently trying to hide His true meaning from some? Jesus responded:

> *To you has been entrusted the mystery of the kingdom of God [that is, the secret counsels of God which are hidden from the ungodly]; but for those outside [of our circle] everything becomes a parable.*   Mark 4:11, AMP

Through these parables, Jesus was hiding His truths from those who did not love Him and revealing His truths to those who did. His disciples could understand, but no one else could, because it was not meant for them to understand. There are many who would not understand what God is saying here in these pages, and they may not even read them because it is not their time to be released in the earth.

These revelations were not intended for everyone. They were not meant for all to understand. Although others might read them, the meaning may well be hidden to them.

So why are you and I given this privilege? Why are we doing Kingdom business together? God sends us His revelation to propel us forward toward the works He has destined us to accomplish in His name. His revelation leads us to His plans and purposes for our lives.

Martin Luther's Privy in the Privy

I am reminded of Martin Luther, the great reformer. He found himself spiritually on the backside of the des-

The Activation of the Seed

ert and made a determination to exert one last effort to change things. He would attend a ministers' conference, where he hoped to find something new and fresh for his life and ministry. He was so discouraged with things as they existed that as he went his way toward that meeting, he was telling God that unless something changed he intended to leave the ministry altogether. It was indeed a critical moment. Strangely, Martin Luther's moment of revelation that would not only change him, but would also change the face of Christianity, came to him while he was in the local privy.

Most of you who are older will know what a privy is, but younger readers may not. It was an outhouse, an outdoor pit toilet. At home we might call it a bathroom, but out in public we say "rest room." That's what a privy was, and Martin Luther was visiting one that day.

As he did this, he was not a happy man. The meetings seemed to be just more of the same old rhetoric and church politics, and he was so spiritually dry that he felt like he was spitting out sand. "God, what are we missing?" he prayed, as he entered the privy and sat on the privy. He felt like giving up.

Then suddenly, in that privy, on that privy, Martin Luther was given privy. What is this privy that he was being given? This kind of privy means privileged information. God, all of a sudden, began to give Martin Luther revelation that had been hidden in the Word of God until that moment. It was always there in the Word, but it was hidden from the eyes of man.

Understanding the Seed

SECRET OR WITHDRAWN

Privy, used in this sense, means "secret or withheld." In a spiritual sense, it means that you have been allowed into the King's secret chamber, and something not meant to be made known to others has been granted to you, and is suddenly deposited into your spirit man. People can be all around you, standing next to you, and if they have not stood in the secret chamber of our King, they will never been given the revelation you have just received. Therefore you are a possessor of privileged information.

Suddenly, a revelation came forth to Martin Luther: *"The just shall live by faith."* Those few words from Heaven turned the world upside down and inside out, and we are still walking in that revelation today. The mighty Reformation came about as a result of someone hearing the voice of God. And the revelation or the privy came in the privy.

So not everyone will get what we are revealing here in these pages. You are receiving privileged information that will catapult you to a higher level of ministry. A great shift is about to take place in your life.

Before my husband and I knew that we would be attending the annual Ministers' and Workers' Convention at Calvary Campground, God began to place this word in my spirit for those meetings (and now for you through the pages of this book). We were actually preparing to attend the funeral of John R. Chappell there, when my husband went to the camp website and noticed that the ministers' meeting was to start a few days later. We knew immediately that we wanted to be there. We didn't know that we would be speaking, but when God speaks prophetically, He moves in mysterious ways.

I pray that every word the Father has placed in my heart for you may go forth, being sown into your hearts. When a proper seed is sown into proper soil, the birds of the air cannot come and carry it away. In another spelling and use of the word, *sewn*, I pray that the seed will be *sewn*, stitched with needle and thread, into your spirits, so that it can never depart.

MY CONNECTION TO THE ASHLAND CAMPGROUND

My connection to the Ashland campground began in 1998 with divine appointments with Sister Ruth Ward Heflin. I soon visited her home and church in Israel. In those days God was opening the windows over my life and ministry and giving us experiences and showing us things that we could only have imagined. Until that time, the word *glory* had remained an intangible thing. The revelation that the prophet Habakkuk received had not yet come to the earth. We were all crying out, "Lord, show us Your glory," but we had no idea what exactly would happen as a result of that prayer. Then, as the Lord opened the windows of Heaven over us, the most amazing and phenomenal things we could ever imagine began to manifest in our meetings. Every time I was around Ruth, those divine appointments turned into divine encounters.

Then, in the year 2000, I began to have divine encounters with Pastor Jane Lowder. I was blessed to meet her in New Orleans, when she came our area to speak in a conference, and that divine appointment turned into a divine encounter. Since then, our relationship has been a blessing.

God's Surprises

Many times you and I have no clear concept of exactly what God has in store for us, and there's a reason for that. He delights in surprising us.

In considering the story of the widow woman and Elijah, it all began when he prophesied to the elements, they obeyed him, and no rain fell for the next three and a half years. This happened because the wicked King Ahab and his wicked Queen Jezebel were on the throne in Israel. God had issues with Ahab before he ever married Jezebel. He was an idolater, a sun worshipper, and he ruled wickedly, but when he married Jezebel, that was just the final straw. Now God had to do something to get Ahab's attention, and he used Elijah to do it.

After these dramatic events, you would think that Elijah's ministry would be taking off, but just the opposite happened. He was now sent to hide along the brook Cherith, the place of cutting away. He drank from the stream (until that dried up), and the ravens came and fed him every day.

When the brook began to dry up, God said to Elijah, "I am now sending you to Zarephath (the place of refinement), and I have prepared a widow woman there who will sustain you." In that moment, this woman was totally oblivious to what was about to take place in her life. I say this because often we, too, are totally oblivious to what God is about to do.

God had prepared a widow woman to provide for Elijah. She would be a blessing to him, and he would be a blessing to her. At that moment, however, she had no idea that all of this would happen, and she was out picking up sticks, preparing to cook her last meal and get ready for the seemingly-inevitable death that she and her son would suffer. She was at the point of desperation and did not know that God had prepared her for something great and important. And, believe me, it's the same with us. God has something wonderful prepared for each of us. This woman was about to experience an opportunity to escape from her despair and enter into blessing, and the same door of opportunity is open to you and me today.

An Opportunity to Align with the Prophetic

Arriving in Zarephath, the prophet spoke to the woman, asking her if she could help him with some food. She told him her story. She not only could not help him; she had just enough for one last meal for herself and her son, and then they would soon die. Little did she know that this was her opportunity to get connected to what God was about to do. This was her opportunity to align herself with the prophetic voice of her day, and in the process, fall into favor with God. I don't know about you, but I've been aligning myself with the prophetic voice of the hour, and I sense something about to shift.

Some of you may be reading this as a last-ditch effort to touch God before your world falls apart. Things have not been going well for you, and you seem to be nearing the end. At least that's how you have felt. But God has other ideas for your life. You are not destined for despair, but rather, to the glory of God. He has a divine purpose in mind for your future. Your life will not end as you feared, in total defeat. You will be used for His glory.

In picking up this book, you may have felt like Martin Luther, that ministry was more trouble than it was worth, and that nothing exciting or worthy of note was happening in your life. But you didn't know what God had waiting for you around the next corner.

This woman got connected with the prophetic, connected with what God was doing, and death was no longer her destiny. Instead, she was soon to know prosperity and the blessing of God. Every time I have gone to Calvary Campground, this is what has happened to me. Many prophetic words have been spoken over my life in other places, and yet I could not comprehend the fullness of them until I stepped into the camp waters and began to swim.

When you have a divine encounter with someone like Ruth Ward Heflin or Jane Lowder, they are so full of the Spirit of God that you begin to encounter Him in a new way, just by meeting them, and your life is forever changed. Every time I had one of those encounters I was so changed that I made it a point that whenever I was about to conduct an important conference or to do some other important meetings in the Kingdom, I made a trip to Ashland (all the way from Baton Rouge, Louisiana), so that I could walk in a fresh flow of the Spirit of God as I went forth.

And some of you will never be the same after reading these pages. I can tell you with an assurance that during the ministers' convention where these messages were first spoken, I stepped into something I had been waiting for for many years. The night when Pastor Peter challenged us to sow our seed into the ground, something sprung up on the inside of me that I had not felt for twelve years. I began to sense my Redeeming Kinsman. Even though I had declared the word of it and spoken the truth of it, the reality of who my Adonai is came over me. These are simple truths that we are exploring, and yet they have the power to catapult or propel you into your destiny.

What Sowing a Seed Really Means

I want us to look now at Genesis 26:12, a passage that has been used already several times in the previous pages, and we have all heard it many times before. Although it is very familiar to us, I pray that we may receive a new revelation of it, so that even our concept of sowing is changed:

> *Then Isaac sowed seed in that land and received in the same year a hundred times as much as he had planted, and the Lord favored him with blessings. And the man became*

Understanding the Seed

great and gained more and more until he became very wealthy and distinguished.
Genesis 26:12-13, AMP

Isaac sowed seed in the land and he received. When we sow seed, something is put into motion, and we receive something back. Something happens instantaneously, and even though you cannot see the fruit of it yet, there is an immediate action that takes place on your behalf. According to *Strong's Concordance*, one of the meanings of the word *sow* is "to be fructified." In other words, as soon as that seed leaves your hand, you become fruitful, you are fructified. Something happens to you. A fruitful process has begun immediately.

The moment you sow an offering to the Lord, something happens. It may not be visible yet, but it is no less real. The process has been set in motion.

When you take the time and make the effort to worship God, you are sowing seeds that are so powerful they will eventually reap a harvest. The moment those seeds of praise leave your mouth, you are fructified. Something begins to happen the moment that seed hits the ground, and it causes you to become fruitful.

Too often, as we sow our seeds, whatever they might be, we are not aware of what has been set in motion. We are not consciously aware of what God is doing because of the sowing of our seed. In that very moment, you are fructified. You are made fruitful, and something is on its way back to you.

The Activation of the Seed

Placing a seed into the ground causes the conception of something you've never had before, and it happens immediately. It may take time for you to see and understand or appreciate the end result, but it's been there since the moment of your sowing.

Sowing means that knowledge comes to you, revelation of things you have never been able to understand. A supernatural action begins to take place the moment your seed goes into the soil.

Living It Qualifies Me To Teach It

Let me deviate a moment here to say that when I teach something, it's because I have first partaken of it myself. I don't just pick something that sounds good to me from the Bible and then share it with others. When I teach, it's because I have lived out what I'm teaching and know personally that it works.

And it's not just that I have lived it. I have also died in it (if you know what I mean by that). This has qualified me to speak it to others. I don't say that in any sense of arrogance, but rather with all humility. I can convey it to you because I have walked it and lived it myself.

Sowing Produces an Immediate Result

When we sow a seed, any seed, something immediately begins to happen on the inside of us. Be aware of it from this day forward. How could we not be aware of it when we saw what happened in those ministers' meetings? Back in the 1980s, God spoke to me about raising up an army in the land. I had not understood exactly how it would happen, but as I stood in Calvary Campground that week, I saw it happening before my very eyes. As Pastor Peter and the other speakers were mightily used by God to declare His Word and that Word went forth, a part of His mighty army was being loosed into the earth to do the work of the Captain of the Hosts.

When you sow, you are fructified. Some fruit immediately begins to develop. Something is conceived, and it begins to grow toward its ultimate harvest. You receive new knowledge and revelation. This all happens the moment you sow into God's Kingdom.

God's Word declares that when Isaac sowed, he reaped. He reaped a hundredfold, and when I sowed my seed the night Pastor Peter spoke to us to do it, I sensed that I would reap a hundredfold harvest from it. I am standing at the door of my destiny, and you can say the same today.

There was a reason you were called into the Kingdom of God. It was declared before the foundations of the earth, when your name was spoken. I believe that with every fiber of my being. At the very foundations of the earth, our names were uttered by God, the Creator of all things. He spoke you and me into existence, and it wasn't just to play house. In that moment He declared what we would do for His glory, the unique part we would play in His divine drama of the ages. You are standing at the door of your destiny in this moment, and a hundredfold blessing will be your portion as you begin to understand the seed and the sowing of your life into the land.

THE ACTIVATION OF THE SEED

WHAT ELSE WAS GRANTED?

What else was granted to Isaac for his faithful sowing? *"The Lord favored him with blessings."* Wow!

Psalm 102:13 is one of my favorite passages of scripture. There the psalmist said:

You will arise and have mercy and loving-kindness for Zion, for it is time to have pity and compassion for her; yes, the set time has come [the moment designated]. AMP

There is a set time, a designated moment, and the psalmist said, *"The set time has come."*

All of the major and minor prophets of the Old Testament books were connected in some way to the Babylonian captivity my husband spoke of in the previous chapter, and their message was that the Israelites, God's people, were coming out of captivity. I declare to you today through the pages of this book that you, too, are coming out of your captivity.

What the psalmist was saying, in Psalm 102:13, was parallel to what Isaiah prophesied concerning the people coming out of Babylonian captivity. Isaiah declared to them that as they came out, they should not expect God to do things in the same old way. He was about to do *"a new thing"*:

Behold, I am doing a new thing! Now it springs forth; do you not perceive and know it and will you not give heed to it? I will even make a way in the wilderness and rivers in the desert.   Isaiah 42:19, AMP

Things will no longer look the way they used to look. This new thing will not feel like the things of God used to feel. It's a new day, and God is doing a new thing. He *"will even make a way in the wilderness and rivers in the desert."* That's significant.

While serving as a missionary to Mexico, I walked in the deserts, to lead people who lived there to the Lord, and I know what it is to be in temperatures up to 118°. Let me tell you: There is no water in the desert. But God will make a way, and waters will spring forth even in the desert places.

In Psalm 102:13, the psalmist is saying the same thing. The King James Version says it this way:

Thou shalt arise, and have mercy upon Zion: for the time to favour her, yea, the set time, is come.

The set time has come, the time that the favor of God will rest upon you.

Isaac had sowed some seed, and the result was that he became fructified. He had a conception. He reaped a hundredfold, and the favor of God was now his portion.

JOB ALSO HAD THIS REVELATION

Job said basically the same thing:

O that thou wouldest hide me in the grave, that thou wouldest keep me secret, until thy wrath be past, that thou wouldest appoint me a set time, and remember me! If a

man die, shall he live again? all the days of my appointed time will I wait, till my change come.
Job 14:13-14, AMP

Job was willing to wait because he knew that God had a set time to come and favor him. Hear me: This is your time to be favored by God, and sowing will cause you to be highly favored.

What Came Next?

What came next for Isaac? *"And the man became great."* Let me declare to you that there is greatness hidden in you. I have always loved to speak of destiny and the seeds of greatness hidden on the inside of people just waiting to come forth. Something special is happening among those who are hungry for God. The greatness in you will come forth, and some of you will be elevated to high positions in the Kingdom of God. Some of you very well may be generals. You just haven't known it.

The mantle of the prophet and the apostle shall rest upon the shoulders of many of you. You just haven't known it until now. You may have been moving toward it, but it has not yet fallen fully upon you. God says that it will surely come. God has divinely ordered our footsteps to bring these timely messages to print. Greatness comes with sowing. Have you sowed your seed?

Understanding the Seed

Something More Happened to Isaac

What else happened to Isaac? He *"gained more and more until he became very wealthy and distinguished."* This word *wealth* can be deceptive. We can be the richest people on the face of the earth without having a lot of earthly riches. This kind of wealth has nothing to do with finances or the lack of them.

Like Isaac, God wants you to become *"distinguished."* You will stand tall among those around you. Believe God for it.

How Can the Dead Be Raised?

The apostle Paul wrote to the Corinthians:

But someone will say, How can the dead be raised? With what [kind of] body will they come forth?
1 Corinthians 15:35, AMP

"How can the dead be raised?" Did any of you feel dead when you started reading this book?

"With what [kind of] body will they come forth?" When a seed goes into the soil and dies, it looks nothing like it will look when it springs forth from that same ground in new life. This is an important point.

A Seed Looks Nothing Like the Fruit It Will Produce

What Paul has written here may well refer to the end-times, when the dead in Christ will be raised and their

The Activation of the Seed

physical bodies will be transformed, but it means something more to us. Paul continued:

You foolish man! Every time you plant seed, you sow something that does not come to life [germinating, springing up, and growing] unless it dies first.
1 Corinthians 15:36, AMP

As we know, a seed must first die before it can bring forth new life. He continued:

Nor is the seed you sow then the body which it is going to have [later], but it is a naked kernel, perhaps of wheat or some of the rest of the grains. 1 Corinthians 15: 7

When it is sown and then dies, a seed looks nothing like the plant it will produce. We need to get excited because we have sown our seed, and we can now expect to see what fruit it will produce. That fruit will amaze us all. The seed has one look when it is sown, but when the harvest comes, what is produced is something wonderfully different. You will not walk or talk the same in the days ahead.

Transformed

Paul continued:

But God gives to it the body that He plans and sees fit, and to each kind of seed a body of its own. 1 Corinthians 15:38

God gives us the body He has planned and sees fit. This represents a mighty transformation that is about to take place. If you put your seed in the ground, you will soon not even resemble that seed. You will be so transformed that you won't even know yourself. Something has happened in the Spirit realm, and the result will be that you look so different people will not be sure you're the same person at all.

You will not only look different; you will also walk differently and talk differently. And it will be because God has given you the body that fits you and suits Him. That should make us all shout.

When a new mantle comes upon you and an office is executed over you, suddenly people will not believe who you have become. They will hardly be able to believe where you came from and what all God has done on your behalf. That transformation has already started. Your seed is germinating and is about ready to pop through the earth, and when it happens you will no longer be the same.

God Always Has a Plan

When God made a covenant with Abraham, Isaac, and Jacob, He had a plan. When Jacob and his descendants went into Egypt and lived in bondage to the Pharaohs for 452 years, God raised up a deliverer for them. Their lives, at that point, seemed chaotic, but in the language of our day, God said to them:

Hang in there with Me. You will go through bitterness, and you will go through unbelief, but My glory will be there in the midst of all of it, and I will carry you past every obstacle and on to the Promised Land. If you will just hang in there with Me, I promise you that when you march into that blessed land, you will not look the same. You have come out of Egypt as a motley group of slaves, but you will march into the land as a kingdom of priests, totally changed for My glory.

Clothed Anew

The people of Israel had come out of Egypt in rags, but they would march into the land clothed as royalty. And God is now changing your garments, too.

When the priesthood was established in the land of Canaan, one of the regulations was that they could not be clothed in wool. They had to wear linen garments. Wool would have caused them to perspire, representing human effort. What God is calling you to do needs to be a "no sweat" situation. No human effort can be involved. God is therefore placing fine linen on you and me today. Why? Because what will happen will not be caused by our human strength. He will do the work. We are just His instruments.

Don't misunderstand what I'm saying. All of us will be called upon to work hard for God in the days ahead, but it will be a "no sweat" situation. God will do it, not you. He does it for His glory. You are clothed in fine linen. You could do nothing to make it happen. Only God could do this.

THE IMPORTANCE OF THRESHOLDS

As we were on our way to the ministers' convention, God began to speak to me about thresholds and showed me that we would be stepping over some of them during those days. Paul wrote to the Corinthians:

> *A wide door of opportunity for effectual [service] has opened to me [there, a great and promising one], and [there are] many adversaries.*   1 Corinthians 16:9, AMP

Every effectual door that was opened to Paul was also surrounded by many enemies. That should not surprise us. We experience it too. Just as we do, Paul struggled with finances, with sickness, and with every other possible type of hindrance. Like Elijah, Paul was *"a man subject to like passions as we are"* (James 5:17).

This helps us. Expect every effectual door opened to you to be surrounded by many adversaries. That's not to inject negativism into the equation. It's to understand the reality of the kingdom struggle. If you know what to expect, you'll know how to react, so that you can continue to be catapulted into ever higher levels of spiritual service.

THE ANCIENT GUARDIANS OF THE THRESHOLDS

The story of Queen Esther, found in the book that also bears her name, is true, but it is also an allegory and can teach us many things. Her uncle Mordecai, a type of the Holy Spirit, was honored to sit at the gates of the city (see Esther 2:21). It was a strategic position. The gate was not only an important place of business; it was also there, in the gate, where all political decisions were made. The respected elders of the land met there on a regular basis.

One of the meanings of the word *gate*, according to the concordance, was "the place of resorting to God for help." Those gates were the threshold to the entire kingdom.

In ancient times, there were eunuchs, also called king's chamberlains, who were assigned to guard the threshold. They became known as "the Guardians of the Threshold." In the time of King Ahasuerus, two of these men, named Bigthan and Teresh, for some reason turned against the king and thought to do him harm. This king was a type or shadow of our God, so this was serious.

This evil plot became known to Mordecai because of his activities at the gates, he relayed the news of it to Esther, and she passed it along to the king. In this way, because of the sensitivity and loyalty of Mordecai, a type of the Holy Spirit, the treachery of the two men was uncovered, and they were hanged. A note about it was entered into the official Book of the Chronicles.

I should say here that there has always been a plot in the heart of Satan to kill the seed before it can bear fruit. This is not to say that his plot will succeed. God's Word promises:

No weapon that is formed against thee shall prosper.
                                            Isaiah 54:17

Satan's weapons shall not prosper, but this doesn't mean that such a weapon has not been formed. It has been formed, but it will not prosper. I've seen these weapons being formed against me, but I also have God's promise that they will not prosper.

There is an assignment in the earth to kill the seed. Why? Because if the seed is killed, it stops the move of God. If the seed that God has placed in you can be killed, the enemy will feel that he has succeeded in stopping God's plans and purposes. That was what moved Bigthan and Teresh to evil. They were entrusted with guarding the threshold and preventing the entrance of unwanted enemies, but they turned on the king and wanted to stop the seed. If they could kill the seed, they could stop the progress of the kingdom.

Haman's Evil Plot

You remember Haman. He had the same spirit. He wanted to destroy all the Jewish people in the kingdom. Unfortunately, Chapter 3 of Esther records the fact that Haman was able to worm his way into the good graces of the king, and the king, not realizing what an evil man Haman was, elevated him above the other princes of the kingdom and ordered all others to bow down to him. Like Lucifer, his father, Haman wanted all the glory.

It was revelation knowledge, transferred from Mordecai (representing the Holy Spirit) to Esther (representing the Bride of Christ), that prevented the plot of Bigthan and Teresh from succeeding, and now Haman had a similar plot. From this day forward, God will enlighten you with revelation, and as the attacks of the enemy come to try to destroy the seed in you, God will give you victory over the evil one. God has already confirmed to you that the seed cannot be killed. It will live and produce fruit.

The Same Spirit

The spirit that drove Haman was the same spirit that was in Adolf Hitler when he set about to annihilate the Jews of Europe. This was the same spirit that drove the Pharaoh of Moses' day to have all of the male Jewish babies killed, the same spirit that drove Herod to have all the babies of Jesus' day two years old and under slaughtered. It was the same spirit that was in Judas, when he tried to have Jesus destroyed.

It was that same Anti-Christ spirit that crucified Jesus. The enemy thought that if he could just kill Jesus, in other words, kill the seed, he would kill the plans and purposes of God. And Satan has the same thought concerning you today. If he can kill the seed God has placed in you, he thinks he can stop you from doing anything for God. But he is a liar. You and I are destined for greater things in the earth.

The Fullness of Time

Jesus started His ministry in *"the fullness of time"* (Galatians 4:4). You may have been in the ministry now for a long time. I've been in it for years myself. But I am convinced that the fullness of time has not yet come for me. I know what it is to be on the edge of it and wait for it to come, but now our time is quickly approaching.

There were many times in the past that I knew I was on my way to the King's palace. I could smell the bread baking, and yet it was put off until another time. Get ready, beloved. Our time has come.

Amen!

CHAPTER 9

UNDERSTANDING THE SEED, PART III
BY PASTOR PETER KANGE

As servants of God, we must know how to manage His presence in public places. We must be mature enough to help others mature, without muzzling and smothering them. Some revivals have broken out and then quickly fizzled because of a lack of wisdom on the part of the servants involved. That surely wasn't God's fault. It was the people who rejected His knowledge, and when we reject His knowledge, God rejects us from being His priests and looks for others who are better able to represent Him. It's not that ministry ceases, but it ceases in the same depth. None of us wants that.

Before there can ever be ministry to people, there must be ministry to the Lord. If we have not learned to walk with Him and commune with Him on a regular basis, then we are not qualified to minister to others. One of the best things we can do to prepare ourselves in this regard is pray in the Holy Ghost, and again I encourage you to do it.

Understanding the Seed

Praying in the Spirit Is a Wise Investment

Why bother to pray in the Spirit? More of us in ministry need to have a business mindset. If we invest in something, then there will be a return. If we invest little, our return will be small. If we invest much, it will be great. This was the reason Paul declared:

I thank my God, I speak with tongues more than ye all.
1 Corinthians 14:18

Paul knew a good investment when he saw it, and we know what he accomplished as a result. If more of God's people could think of prayer in the sense of investing and reaping a reward on that investment, we would spend much more time calling on God in the Spirit. If you invest nothing at all, what do you reap? The answer, of course, is nothing at all.

It is sad that many modern-day Christians have the idea that once they have been born again, they can just sit back and do nothing, waiting for the Lord to do everything. God insists, in His Word, that there must be works with our faith. You simply cannot separate the two.

Too many Christians refuse to pray and refuse to fast. They think they have great faith, and they are just sitting waiting for God to do something. In the meantime, they themselves are doing nothing. In spite of the fact that they are doing nothing, they still expect a lot from the Lord. I'm not sure where this concept came from, but I'm convinced that it is a lie from the pits of Hell. It is an attack against your prosperity, an attack against your increase.

Is it possible to not go to work and still get a paycheck? I don't think so. Why is it then that those who fail to fast and pray are still expecting a paycheck from God? Some say, "I fasted and prayed already. I'm tired." Really? No paycheck for you.

A System of Rewards

Like it or not, we are employed in a system of rewards. Do X, and God will bless you for it. So the outcome is predictable. It is exactly the same as in the business world.

Some months ago, I was dealing with a young man. I asked him if he was willing to invest toward his future. He said he was.

"Do you really want to increase?" I asked him.

"Oh, yes," he responded.

"Okay, then," I told him, "I'll make a bargain with you. I want you to invest $_____ in your future. If you are willing to do that, I will work with you over the next two weeks. If you don't get more back than you've invested, I'll refund your investment." Why would I do that? Because the outcome was predictable.

You are the seed of God, and the outcome of the life He has planted in you is predictable. When you plant a seed in the ground, the outcome is predictable. You do what you are supposed to do, and you get what you deserve.

Everything we do has a proper and improper way to be done. Do it the right way, and the results will be good.

Fail to do it right, and there are no guarantees. It is not just a matter of having the right thoughts or the right heart intention. You have to do the actual works.

In order to accomplish certain things in life, we must move parts of our bodies, and unless we do, nothing happens. You have to move, and it is now time for us to move forward.

Accomplishing Anything of Consequence in Life Requires Action on Your Part

Accomplishing anything of consequence in life requires work on your part. It requires your involvement. If you don't do anything, you can't complain about not getting your share of the benefits. Nothing in life is free, not even Heaven. You have to get plugged into the system.

What do I mean by that? Well, systems are created to give us guidelines about what is expected of us. Certain systems require a certain pattern of behavior. For instance, there's the American credit system. If you fail to appreciate the system and to make your payments on time, you lose your good credit rating. If you pay your bills on time, you receive a good credit rating. It's as simple as that. A certain action leads to a certain consequence.

Understanding God's System

The Kingdom of God also works on a system. There are various components in God's arrangement of things, and when you understand the purpose of every component, you will treat it with the dignity it deserves.

Understanding the Seed, Part III

Think, for instance, about having an automobile, but forgetting to have enough gasoline for it. What would be the point? It would do you no good at all. You might as well park it and not plan to go anywhere with it.

You could desire to drive it all you want. You might even fast and pray about it. But if you were still missing that important component (gasoline), the car would stay right where it was, and you would get nowhere. It's the same with faith and works.

A Problem of Balance

We seem to have this balance problem in many areas. When God begins to talk to us about faith, we all move toward faith and neglect the love component of the Gospel. Then, when we start emphasizing the love component, we forget the giving component. All of these things work together.

The Word of God says in the book of Isaiah:

Seek ye out of the book of the LORD, and read: no one of these shall fail, none shall want her mate: for my mouth it hath commanded, and his spirit it hath gathered them.
Isaiah 34:16

What did God mean when He said, "*None shall want her mate?*" Can you imagine that God, who wrote His Word, would forget His hand and give you His leg? Join the leg and accomplish all things, for they all work together.

You might pray and fast for blessings and pray and fast for your ministry, but if you ignore the importance of having a good word in your mouth, and you are backbiting other people, you will not get far in God. The anointing will take you places where character is needed if you are to stand. (Yes, this all has to do with the seed.)

One day, not too long ago, the Lord came to me and asked me what I was doing. I wasn't sure what He meant. He said, "Seed, what are you doing? I didn't put that in you, so why are you doing that? Is that what you are trying to produce? If that is not what you are trying to produce, then don't do it." I stopped what I was doing immediately.

God's system is wonderful, but His Word warns us that when we do not know how to use it properly, we confuse the angels, and they can actually begin to destroy the works of our hands (Ecclesiastes 5:6). We must know how to handle what God has given us.

Since systems are created to produce a certain behavioral pattern, if we plug into that system, we can know what will be the outcome. Get plugged into God's system today, and you'll reap His rewards.

Learn To See Beyond What Is Right In Front of You

The events of the coming years, brothers and sisters, will work together for our benefit. It is God's desire to have His people see beyond what's right in front of them, so He is revealing things to us by His Spirit.

Understanding the Seed, Part III

In His Word, He declares:

Genesis 22:15-17
> [15] *And the angel of the Lord called unto Abraham out of heaven the second time,* [16] *and said, By myself have I sworn, saith the Lord, for because thou hast done this thing, and hast not withheld thy son, thine only son:* [17] *that in blessing I will bless thee, and in multiplying I will multiply thy seed as the stars of the heaven, and as the sand which is upon the sea shore; and thy seed shall possess the gate of his enemies.*

Was God just talking about sand here? No, He was talking about you and me. We are the ones who will possess the gates of the enemy.

The day I preached this message in the ministers' convention at Calvary Campground, I woke up from a dream. In my dream there was a huge gate, and I climbed over it and went to speak with a man living in a mansion behind it.

"Why are you here?" he asked. "You're not supposed to be here!" And he repeated his question several times over: "Why are you here? Why are you here?"

I smiled and said, "I've done the work it takes to be here. That's why I'm here." I had climbed over that gate. If you fail to do what is required to stand on a certain platform, then you are an impostor.

You might say, "But no one has even given me the opportunity to preach." Okay, but be sure you are not doing what imposters do.

I kept insisting to the man that I belonged there, and he kept insisting that I didn't. I said, "But I paid the price," and that seemed to settle the issue.

For quite some time, I had been speaking wealth and riches over our lives. I had been declaring that we were above average when it came to wealth. When anyone gave me a prophetic word concerning finances, I never once objected that it was "too much." Instead, I said, "Yes! Yes! Yes!"

I paid the price to be there, and we must all do whatever it takes to get there. Climb, and don't stop when you are halfway there. Some seem to be saying, "I've come a long way. Let me rest now." Others are saying, "I don't think this is God's route for me; it's too tedious." The Scriptures say:

> *And Jesus said unto him, No man, having put his hand to the plough, and looking back, is fit for the kingdom of God.*   Luke 9:62

It's Seedtime

God said it. I didn't. Get with the system.

It is seedtime, beloved, time for the seed, time for the saints. It's your time. This is your season. Don't ever believe that this is a tired cliché. It's not.

This is your season. This is your time. It's seedtime, but you must know how to act as an appropriate seed.

When it is rainy season, what does the rain do? It comes down, doesn't it. It takes advantage of its season.

Understanding the Seed, Part III

When it's the hot, growing season, can you hide the sun or prevent the temperatures outside from rising? Of course, the severity of it will depend on where you are in the world, but summer usually means high temperatures. It's just the season for it.

It's seedtime, the season for the seed, your time to flourish, and when it's your season, that means you are in the ground. Now, you can no longer remain in the dormant stage. You have been planted, and you must begin to grow. You are quickly moving toward the goal of producing fruit.

Seedtime and Harvest Depend on Each Other

Seedtime and harvest depend on each other. They go together. Once the seed is put into the ground, a harvest can be anticipated. If there is seed, there will be a harvest. It's guaranteed. Therefore your life is now on auto-play. A harvest is surely coming.

The moment the Holy Ghost drops a seed into your spirit, you can know that it means a harvest is coming. If it is seedtime, then that means harvest will soon follow. So when it's seedtime, begin to look for harvest time too.

Avoid Error

As I look back over my life, I can see how the Lord, at various times, helped me avoid error. When something is done out of sync with the accepted system, that's not good. We are part of a system, and I intend to stay within the system. We must learn to close our ears to what is not of that system. We must discipline ourselves to do what is right. Why? Because we are preparing for a harvest.

Sometimes we are so eager to get something that we dive right in and grab at it, when that may not be what God wants for us at all. Something about it is a little off. Because seedtime determines harvest time, we have to learn what is right and then do what is right.

Harvest Is a Time of Suddenlies

When it's seedtime, things do not seem to be moving swiftly, but harvest time is a period of suddenlies. Things begin to happen quickly.

It's interesting. These suddenlies are only suddenlies in the natural. In the Spirit realm, God has been working behind the scenes for a very long time. There is nothing sudden about it in God. Suddenly a thing springs forth, and people are saying, "Wait a minute. Where did this powerful man of God come from? We have never heard of him before." "Where did this powerful woman come from? We've never heard of her before." Yes, but God has been working behind the scenes on them for a long while. To you, their rise happens suddenly, and a harvest is there to be reaped, but God wasn't taken by surprise. He seeded it all and watched it grow. Now, suddenly, people from all over the world are being raised up with dynamic ministries. These people flow in the prophetic like we have never seen before. They're strange. And, by the way, since

I'm addressing this to seeds, I'm sure, that you are rather strange, too.

The people of Jesus's time said of Him, "Isn't this the carpenter's son?" He was strange to them. They marveled, and so will the people around you. You will be shocked yourself by the way you flow in the Spirit. "My God," you'll declare, "I didn't know all of that was inside of me. Wow! What was that?" Well, that's the strange. That's the new. That's the other.

In the past, I occasionally heard believers saying, "I'm not sure about this thing, whether it's from God or not. Let's just leave it alone for now to be safe." We are going to hear that more and more in the days ahead. This is a season of suddenlies, a season of the new and different, and it will leave some people perplexed and wondering.

Doctrinal Bubbles Burst

In the days ahead, many will find their doctrinal bubbles being burst. God is raising up many new and strange people, and they are doing many new and strange things. We can insist on hanging on to the past, but if we do, at some point, we may find ourselves feeling very lonely. You might as well join the "strange ones."

In the days ahead, you will be joined in relationship to people you didn't even like before. They will come into alignment with you because they notice that you already have what God is currently talking about. They will cling to you, pleading, "Please take us in. We know you have it. Teach us about it."

Go with the Flow

Some time ago, the Lord had me teach on the Holy Spirit and His gifts, but He warned me not to teach what I had taught in the past. We're now talking about a move of God and the manifestations of the Spirit within that particular move. Not one of us can now say, "This is my gift, and I will remain in it." We don't know how things will go tomorrow or next week, so we have to go with the flow.

If the Spirit begins to move prophetically, then we must go prophetic. If the flow of the Spirit goes toward the word of knowledge, then we must go with the word of knowledge. If it goes with the word of wisdom, then we are to go with the word of wisdom. If it is suddenly with the gift of faith, then we must flow with the gift of faith. However God chooses to go, that is how we must flow.

I can hear many saying, "Well, God didn't call me to do that, so I don't want to get involved." Well, have it your way, but you are missing out on so much. It's time to get out of your corner and move forward. Because of the things that are coming, you will have to move forward if you want to flow with God.

"Make Up Your Mind to Move Forward"

In 2010, the Lord spoke to me and said, "Make up your mind to move forward, and I will bring you to the front."

Understanding the Seed, Part III

Well, now that some years have passed, I have a different understanding of that than I did at the time. I thought I *had* moved forward and *was* moving forward, but what is happening right now is *really* moving forward.

Moving forward is a move. *Move* and *forward*, of course, are two very different words, but when they are put together they have a very interesting meaning. I looked up the word *forward*, and I noticed something amazing. *Forward*, in itself, seems to suggest movement. Why, then, would God put the two words together?

As I kept studying the word *forward*, I noticed that it can also be a position more than an action. So when God says to us, "Move forward," He is looking at something definite. He is saying, "Take yourself in that direction." It's time to move forward.

You might ask, "Where am I moving to?" Well, a forward movement can only be ahead. It is never backward.

Move forward also denotes a quickness. Move on to a new place in God, and do it quickly.

Cancel All Delays

If God is speaking to us of moving forward, and He is bringing to us a time of the suddenlies, this means that He is now canceling all delays. No more delays. Miracles will now happen instantly. They will happen right now. There can be no more delays.

You and I are in a move of God. Why can we say that this is a move of God? Because we see Him releasing soldiers into the battlefield. These are not confused and poorly prepared people. God has given them specific direction and specific preparation.

Specific Instructions

As we move ahead, we, too, will be given (and will also give to others) very specific instructions. We are even now in a time of instruction, and we must learn how important such instruction is.

"Sit down" means sit down. It does not mean sit physically, but remain standing on the inside. God is setting us free to be completely obedient to Him. This is a time for instruction, a time to prepare for the suddenlies.

God is moving quickly. If He says, "Now," that doesn't mean wait some more. It doesn't mean hold on a little longer. "Now" is the call for immediate action, and we must respond. How else will we possess the gate of the enemy? Believe me, if you haven't learned how to act now, you will quickly be left behind.

So many Christians have rested in the statement, "I'm just waiting on the Lord," but suddenly that statement has grown stale and tired. This is not a time for waiting; it is a time for action. When we ask someone to do something in the church and their response is, "I'm not really ready for that yet," they are failing to recognize what a wonderful opportunity has been presented to them, and they are allowing it to pass them by. When we are invited to do something for God or His people, it means that a new door has opened for us, and God's grace is available to us to pass through that door. If we yield to that truth, we are yielding to His grace. Far too many are missing their opportunities.

A Time of Major Decisions

Some of you are about to face major decisions in your life. Get sensitized to the Holy Ghost so that you can flow with what God is saying. I'm addressing myself, as well as you.

When I am faced with a challenge, I don't cry. Crying is not a prescription for victory. Believing God is a prescription for victory. Get plugged in and do what God's system expects.

The Bible shows us that the children of Israel were terrified when they saw Pharaoh approaching:

> *And when Pharaoh drew nigh, the children of Israel lifted up their eyes, and, behold, the Egyptians marched after them; and they were sore afraid: and the children of Israel cried out unto the Lord.*   Exodus 14:10

I pray that God will send Pharaoh to march on you too, so that you will be quickened to move forward in the name of Jesus. That's what Pharaoh did for the children of Israel. They were standing there in front of the Red Sea, but there was no movement. It took Pharaoh coming behind them to move them on. So if Pharaoh doesn't come, the miracle we are waiting for may not happen. Come, Pharaoh, come!

Oh, yes. We need some creditors to call and threaten us so that we can move forward. Come, creditors, come!

We want to possess the gates of our enemies. Come, evil, come! Push us forward. Stir us to move.

Are We Ready?

Are we ready for the devil? Will he find us prepared for once? Will we know what we are talking about this time? There was a time when we feared sickness, but now we must welcome its coming. How shall we raise the dead, if there are no dead to be raised? How shall we lay hands on the sick, if there are no sick to be healed? How shall a fish grant us a coin, if there is no need for money? If nothing is going wrong in your world, then there is nothing to fix. If nothing terrible is happening to you, then there is no need for faith. This is a season for faith, and that means it is also a season for works, and the result is that many needs will be cropping up and will require the exercise of your faith. Get ready for it.

"They Were Sore Afraid"

What was the reaction of the children of Israel as Pharaoh approached? *"They were sore afraid."* In the days ahead, we cannot afford to be governed by our passions. God's Word declares:

> *Be careful for nothing; but in every thing by prayer and supplication with thanksgiving let your requests be made known unto God.*   Philippians 4:6

We must not allow anything to trouble us. Our response to bad things must be thanksgiving and prayer. Can you effectively thank someone if your spirit is in turmoil. "Oh, God! Oh, God," we cry in utter despair, but that's not prayer. That's emotion, and emotion is never an expression of faith.

Does this mean that we have to be tough? Well, the devil is tough, so, yes, we must be even tougher. He's not playing around with you. His plan is to take you out. Thank God that He will enable us to fulfill His plan to bury the enemy.

Moses Had the Right Answer

Moses had the right answer for the people standing at the Red Sea that day:

And Moses said unto the people, Fear ye not, stand still, and see the salvation of the Lord, which he will shew to you to day: for the Egyptians whom ye have seen to day, ye shall see them again no more for ever. The Lord shall fight for you, and ye shall hold your peace.
Exodus 14:13-14

"Ye shall see them again no more for ever." There is no resurrection in the camp of the enemy. Resurrection belongs only to the people of God.

I was speaking in a hotel once at the inauguration of a new ministry, and I was led to call people out, speak a word of knowledge over them, and pray for them. While

I was doing this, I could hear some sort of commotion outside the room. When I minister, I am very sensitive to what is going on around me. I tried to focus on what I was doing, but I kept hearing that commotion.

Eventually my wife came in and began trying to get my attention. Some people were dragging in a woman who had just died, and they wanted to get me to pray for her.

At first, I didn't waver from what I was doing, and everyone wondered why I was not responding to the need of the dead woman. In my spirit, however, I sensed that every other case there was just as important as hers. A person suffering from a headache needed help, as much as the dead woman.

We cannot categorize miracles as being big or small. Raising the dead is not a bigger miracle than the healing of a headache. They are all on the same level, and the same faith is needed for each. Raising the dead is one of the elementary things Christians should be doing on a regular basis (see Hebrews 6:1).

Pastor Pauline and others were trying to get my attention, as I kept doing what I was doing. Eventually, when I had finished praying for the others, I turned to the dead lady and said, "Get up!" And she got up.

We can believe God and not make things complicated. Just believe Him. Don't entertain arguments inside your head. Don't complicate matters. If you think too much, you make things hard. They become problematic. Just believe God and act accordingly. I don't have a problem praying for Pharaoh to show up. The sooner he shows up, the sooner we can take care of him.

UNDERSTANDING THE SEED, PART III

THEY DID SOME OTHER CRAZY THINGS

The children of Israel *"were sore afraid,"* and they *"cried unto the Lord."* They did some other crazy things:

> *And they said unto Moses, Because there were no graves in Egypt, hast thou taken us away to die in the wilderness? wherefore hast thou dealt thus with us, to carry us forth out of Egypt? Is not this the word that we did tell thee in Egypt, saying, Let us alone, that we may serve the Egyptians? For it had been better for us to serve the Egyptians, than that we should die in the wilderness.*
>
> Exodus 14:11-12

Moses was not the problem, and yet these people now turned on him. They actually said they would have preferred to stay in Egypt. Can you imagine that?

It reminds me of what happened to David. His men, who had been so loyal and willing before, suddenly wanted to stone him. And this could happen to you, too, so you need to be prepared for it. Your precious people, the ones you led to the Lord and helped to get healed, could suddenly turn on you and come after you with a desire to take you out.

What can you do in a case like that? Try to help everyone keep their minds on the real problem. Pharaoh was the problem, not their leaders. Your Pharaoh is surely coming, so get ready.

Facing Pharaoh should never be a problem. There will be many great challenges in the days ahead. Face them all boldly, knowing who you are in Christ. Many storms and floods will come your way. Know that you will be established upon the floods. So let the floods come. We are ready for them. We are ready to possess the gates of our enemies.

Respond to Instructions

Many Christians are still far too resistant to taking instructions. Make up your mind to fully submit yourself to authority, and make up your mind to joyfully receive all instructions you are given. Just as you expect those who follow you to receive your instructions, you must be ready to take instruction from whoever is above you.

Once, when I was preaching a meeting, I called one of the ladies present to come down to the front for personal ministry. The people around her said, "She can't come."

I said, "She can't come?"

Then I said to her, "Come to me."

"No," I was told, "she's had an accident and broken her leg."

I said, "All the more reason that she should come to me." And she got up and walked.

Everyone was amazed. "She's walking." Of course she was walking. My instruction to her had been simple, "Come to me," and such a word is strong enough to mend broken bones.

Issuing such a command doesn't require a booming voice. It requires knowing who you are in Christ.

"Fear Ye Not"

"Let us alone that we may serve the Egyptians," the people had said to Moses. What was wrong with them?

It was then that Moses spoke the words of that powerful verse 13:

> *Fear ye not, stand still, and see the salvation of the LORD, which he will show to you today: for the Egyptians whom ye have seen today, you shall see them no more for ever.*
> Exodus 14:13

I dare you to stand still and see the salvation of the Lord this day. It is seedtime.

"Go Forward"

Now God spoke to Moses:

> *And the LORD said unto Moses, wherefore criest thou unto me. Speak unto the children of Israel that they go forward.*
> Exodus 14:15

Yes, it's time to go forward. In an earlier chapter of the book, we have that wonderful charge:

> *Whatsoever thy hand findeth to do, do it with thy might.*
> Ecclesiastes 9:10

We can all say a hearty amen to this. It's time to go forward. It's time to get involved.

I meet many people who say to me, "I don't know what I'm supposed to do next. Could you please pray and tell me what the Lord is saying." I don't pray such prayers.

I feel like asking them, "What have you done with the thing that is right in front of you?"

When God told Moses to tell the people to move forward, there was a position involved, and there was a destination involved. They needed to start moving in that direction, moving forward. If the Lord has already spoken to you, then what you need to do is keep moving forward in what He has already said until He shows you something else.

God would not have been saying, "Move forward," to these people if He had not shown them some goal to move forward to. They knew where they were supposed to be going. They just needed to get moving forward toward that goal.

I sense that there is a door open before you right this minute, but something else is causing you to wonder if you should really go through it. It's time to stop saying, "I don't know," and start doing what you already know to do. Enough I-don't-knows already! Just move forward.

"I don't know for sure if I should get into this certain business venture," you might say. What made you think of it in the first place? If God spoke to you to do it, how will you know what will happen until you start trying? You are wasting too much time saying, "I don't know," too much time deciding to pray about it. How long do you have to pray?

Have you ever noticed that as long as you keep procrastinating about a matter you never hear from God during all that time? Why do you suppose that is? It must mean that God is not in agreement with your procrastination. He is saying to you, "Move forward."

Understanding the Seed, Part III

When Will You Be Ready?

You were given a first preaching opportunity, and you answered, "I'm not ready." You were given a second opportunity, and you responded, "Let me pray some more about it." When the third opportunity came, you had another excuse. When do you plan to be ready? Can you not get yourself ready? When you receive a word from God, a seed comes into you and makes you a seed, and you can then release yourself into what God is saying, whether you feel ready or not.

I know people who have received specific words like, "Pack your bags; it's time to go," and they still made excuses and said, "Let me pray and know the perfect timing of it." If it's not now, then when? God's instruction was, "Pack your bags!" What else do you need to hear?

"Pack your bags" is not a command for the future. Pack your bags means, go start packing now, and God will reveal the rest.

Do you have what you need for the journey? It doesn't matter. Go pack your bags, and God will take care of the rest. I've had many miracles come to me by just taking God at His word, without thinking or planning. And I can't think of a single miracle that came about through my thinking and planning. May God help us to stop procrastinating and get moving forward.

I have traveled many times on nothing more than a "Let's go" from the Lord, and I have left town with only the clothes on my back, and He provided all that I needed. You thinking about not having the money doesn't get you anywhere. God is wondering what part of what He has said can be interpreted as meaning, "Wait for the money."

No, if He says, "Go to Vietnam," for example, you pack your bags and go to the airport. If there is no flight at the moment and you have to wait, that waiting is understandable. That is a legitimate waiting, but not when you sit and wonder about the timing and the hows and wheres of everything. If you get moving, God will make a way for you.

WE THINK TOO MUCH

When the Lord says, "You will go to the nations," most of us begin to think of what job we can get that will pay enough for us to go to the nations. And that's the problem. We think too much. When the Lord says, "You are going to the nations," answer Him, "Okay. Which one do I start with?" or something positive like that.

Paul was busy doing what he did, when the Holy Ghost spoke to him in a dream and told him not to go the direction he had been planning and sent him off to Macedonia instead. How do you expect the Spirit to give you direction for something new when you are currently doing nothing at all? It's not going to happen.

Peter was busy fishing when the Lord came along and told him that He would make him a fisher of men. You have to be doing something before more direction will come to you.

When Elijah fled into the wilderness because Jezebel was threatening his life, God met him there and asked him, "What are you doing here?" You need to be doing something.

Understanding the Seed, Part III

Reverence the Position of Older Servants

Even after he had been anointed king, David remained under Saul's command. He was greatly used by God to chase evil spirits from Saul, but that didn't entitle him to try to take the king's place.

When God raised up Samuel, the child didn't say, "Eli, you're getting old. I think I should take over, especially since I seem to be having all the visions and dreams." No, Samuel reverenced the position of the older man and could not bear to tell him the negative things God had shown him would happen to the priest and his family.

How I Got Started

When God began to use me, it was not in a church. He had me locked up in my room, and there He taught me worship. There I began to visit Heaven and have many other wonderful experiences. It was there that I learned to hear God's voice. At times, the Lord would tell me the name of people in need, give me directions to their house, and tell me what they were suffering from, so that I could go and minister to them. He gave me a gift that is very similar to seeing an x-ray image.

You don't know what God might want to do through you. You just need to make room for Him to work as He wills. When we are open to Him, He will do through us what is needful for the Kingdom in that moment. Get ready for whatever comes your way.

Don't Build Your Ministry on Gifts

We must be careful because I learned early in my ministry that it could not be built on gifts. I had many people coming to me to know what God was saying at the moment, and the truth was that they had no intention of serving Him. I even had people of other religious beliefs wanting to receive a word from our God but not intending to serve Him. I put a stop to that right away. Everything that we do must glorify God and build His Kingdom. Get ready to flow with God, to know what needs to be said in the moment and to say it to His glory.

Learn Discretion

To be used by God in this way, we must learn discretion. Just because something has been revealed to you doesn't give you license to talk about it. Sometimes God speaks to me as I'm driving and shows me things about other people. Such knowledge can be shared only in the context and timing He indicates. If you misuse the information He gives you, He won't be able to trust you the next time.

Learn the Right Way

There is a right way and a wrong way to do things in God's Kingdom. The right way blesses people and builds the Kingdom. The wrong way hurts people and brings division.

Understanding the Seed, Part III

Jesus taught:

For what shall it profit a man, if he shall gain the whole world, and lose his own soul?   Mark 8:36

It doesn't matter how much you can see in the Spirit; you must not be rebellious with any information God has given you. We are stewards of whatever He tells us, so if He tells you something, and you fail to appropriate it or handle it correctly, who do you suppose He will come after? That's right — you. So you must learn to handle what God shows you.

Sometimes, instead of saying, "God is saying ... ," I phrase my comments as personal advice, and you should be able to receive it. If I have to always say, "God said ... ," in order to get people to receive it, then we have a problem. And we, as ministers, must never start controlling people by using that phrase.

What Should I Do?

A member of our church was determined to do something I was sure God did not want her to do. I turned to God in prayer. "Father," I prayed, "what should I do? I have told her not to do what she is contemplating, but she's not listening."

I was surprised when He answered, "When she makes a trip to check things out, go with her."

I said, "To do what?"

He said, "That's what fathers do."

So I went with her, and we checked everything out, and it seemed great.

"So what's your opinion now?" she asked me. "Wasn't it wonderful?"

"Yes, it was," I had to admit. But that was not the point. I was sure this was not what God wanted for her.

"Is it wonderful?" she asked.

"Yes, it is," I said.

We went back home, and she continued to make her plans. So I went back to prayer. I said, "Father, I made the trip, just like You told me to do."

He said, "Relax! I will do the rest." And to this very day that person has not followed through with her plans.

As ministers, we must learn to say, "If it is the Lord's will, it will come to pass, and if not, then it will not come to pass." Then we have to back this up with the kind of prayer life that assures that if a thing is not the Lord's will it will not come to pass. God will do that for us.

You Don't Need to Do that Right Now

At various times some member has come to me excited about doing something, and I discouraged them: "You don't need to do that right now."

Later, they came back again with a long face, and I said, "If your heart is set on doing it, then go ahead." What can we say? At some point each of us needs to hear God for himself. Each member of the Body of Christ must learn to hear the Master's voice. We certainly don't have time to know every detail for every other person and try to keep them all straight. At some point, they have to grow up and start standing on their own two feet.

"I want to go to Japan," someone may say.

"Okay, when are you coming back?" I would answer.

"Will you pray for me?" they ask.

"Sure. Father, she is going to Japan. Be with her and use her for your glory." I do this because I can't control every detail of my members' lives. It's between her and God. We learn these things in time.

"You Have to Know How to Pastor Judas"

I will never forget what God told me one day in 2010. I was driving along, and He said, "You have to know how to pastor Judas." I remember the exact spot where this happened, and could take you to it today. Suddenly, God's Spirit swept into the car like a wind.

"Why did You come like that?" I asked the Lord.

He said, "I needed to talk to you about something. In fact, I have been trying to talk, and you're not listening."

I said, "Okay." And He began to teach me on the subject of betrayal.

You will remember that Judas kissed Jesus in the garden, but it was a kiss of betrayal. God said that I needed to know how to pastor Judas and not be moved by my emotions.

Think about the horrible thing Judas did to Jesus, and yet our Lord was willing to dine with him, even to wash his feet. Unforgiveness is choking many people in the ministry, and they need to be set free from it.

"The devil is a liar," they say. "I refuse to deal with such people." But we must deal with them. Jesus set the example for us in this regard.

I have met people with huge ministries who are so powerful you would think they are living and sleeping with the Holy Ghost, and yet they refuse to catch a brother when he is falling.

"What did he do?" I ask.

"Well, he has not come clean about his sin," is often their reply.

Come clean to whom? To you? Seriously?

Let me tell you something that may shock you today. None of your church members owes you perfection. If you haven't learned this, you soon will.

They owe God perfection, but not you. You are just human, flesh and blood, as they are. Teach them the Word, and guide them as best you can in God's way. Then leave the rest with God. They are His children, not yours. He has the refiner's fire, and He knows how to use it.

Stop fighting with difficult people. Stop banning certain ones to the back row. And never stop speaking to people because of something they have done. If you will think back, you will realize that your personal life and ministry have often blossomed most when you seemed to be at your weakest point. The Scriptures teach us that God's *"strength is made perfect in weakness"* (2 Corinthians 12:9). God moves when you need Him to move. When you still have other options, He waits for you. Move forward.

Understanding the Seed, Part III

Mix Your Faith with Works

Move forward. Stop contemplating: "Should I build that church building or shouldn't I build it?" Move forward. Build it.

"Should I go out for evangelism or shouldn't I?" Stop waiting. Move forward.

Mix your faith with works. Some say, "I am believing the Lord." That's fine, but now it's time to go lay hands on people. Move forward.

Why is moving forward so important? Because a move of God requires that you be properly positioned. Get into position quickly, for God is about to do a new thing.

Welcome Pharaoh

Before people begin to cry out, "How do we handle this?" let them know early on that Pharaoh will surely come, so they must prepare for his coming. Know in your own soul and declare to others: "Pharaoh is coming," but when he shows up, don't worry about it. God has a plan. Pharaoh is coming, but God is sending miracles to enable us to meet the challenge head-on.

God instructed Moses to stretch forth his rod. That rod spoke of testimonies, of past experiences in God. This was not the first time it had been seen. The people had seen it at other points in their lives, and it had a reputation, a testimony. Now, it was time for that testimony to speak again.

Two orders were given simultaneously: (1) For Moses to tell the people to move forward, and (2) For him to lift up the rod over the sea and divide it. The people could only go forward as Moses exercised his responsibility to divide the sea.

Oh, get ready for it. You will soon be called upon to stretch out your faith and do something you have not done before, and your action of faith will open the way for others to go forward. After you have challenged them to move forward, then it is you who must stand in the place of prayer, lift up your rod, and say, "Sea, my people are coming. Get out of their way." Remove the barrier before you and your people, to enable them to pass over.

"The Sea Saw It and Fled"

The Bible records:

When Israel went out of Egypt, the house of Jacob from a people of strange language; Judah was his sanctuary, and Israel his dominion. The sea saw it, and fled.

Psalm 114:1-3

Wow! Before Moses gave that command and raised his rod, the sea was in its place as usual. But when the sea saw the staff of Moses being raised and the children of Israel determined and beginning to move forward, it fled before them. Praise God! That's what will happen with your enemies too.

Most of you have probably watched the classic film *Ten Commandments* and seen its portrayal of the water of the Red Sea with the fish jumping in and out of it. Is that accurate? Well, the Scriptures say that the water actually stood up like a wall.

What's a wall like? Can you go through a wall? No, right? Well, I want you to realize what God is about to do for us in the twenty-first century. Verse 29 records:

> *But the children of Israel walked upon dry land in the midst of the sea; and the waters were a wall unto them on their right hand, and on their left.*
>
> Exodus 14:29

The night before this, a wind had begun to blow, and it blew all night. The result was that the water stood up as walls. The next chapter, by recording the praise of the people when they had safely reached the other side, tells us much more about this whole affair:

> [3] *The LORD is a man of war: the LORD is his name.*
> [4] *Pharaoh's chariots and his host hath he cast into the sea: his chosen captains also are drowned in the Red sea.*
> [5] *The depths have covered them: they sank into the bottom as a stone.*
> [6] *Thy right hand, O LORD, is become glorious in power: thy right hand, O LORD, hath dashed in pieces the enemy.*
> [7] *And in the greatness of thine excellency thou hast overthrown them that rose up against thee: thou sentest forth thy wrath, which consumed them as stubble.*
> [8] *And with the blast of thy nostrils the waters were gathered together, the floods stood upright as an heap, and the depths were congealed in the heart of the sea.*

> *⁹ The enemy said, I will pursue, I will overtake, I will divide the spoil; my lust shall be satisfied upon them; I will draw my sword, my hand shall destroy them.*
> *¹⁰ Thou didst blow with thy wind, the sea covered them: they sank as lead in the mighty waters.*   Exodus 15:3-10

So what was that wind that blew until the waters of the Red Sea had stood up as walls? It was the blast of the very nostrils of God. Pharaoh was coming, but God was at work, and His miracles were about to be seen. Come, Pharaoh! Come! Come, Pharaoh, because God will answer you Himself with the breath of His nostrils.

In another place, this wind that blew was called *"the east wind,"* and it was the same east wind that brought the quails for the children of Israel to eat in the wilderness.

Let's look at that verse 8 again:

And with the blast of thy nostrils the waters were gathered together, the floods stood upright as an heap.

What is a *heap*? Most of us can visualize a heap of something, but not a heap of water. Water does not normally gather as a heap. As a liquid, it seeks its own level, so it doesn't heap up.

What else does verse 8 say?

And the depths were congealed in the heart of the sea.

What does the word *congealed* mean? According to the *Merriam-Webster Online Dictionary*, *congeal* has these several meanings:

1. to change from a fluid to a solid state by or as if by cold
2. to make viscid or curdled: coagulate
3. to make rigid, fixed, or immobile

Something that is congealed is probably frozen. In the portrayal rendered by the movie *Ten Commandments*, fish were jumping in and out of the water of the Red Sea, but that is probably not the way it happened. If the water stood up as walls and as a heap, it could do so only if it was congealed or frozen.

What does this mean to us today? Everything the enemy has been plotting against you and me is about to be frozen in place.

The Egyptians Slept in Total Darkness

The night before, as the children of Israel camped before the Red Sea, the Egyptians camped nearby. The miraculous pillar of fire God had sent to accompany His children lighted their camp, but the Egyptians slept in total darkness. It may have been at this point that the Lord loosened the wheels of the Egyptian chariots. The next day, as they attempted to cross the Red Sea in pursuit of the Hebrews, those wheels came off. Exodus records:

And [God] took off their chariot wheels. Exodus 14:25

That surely slowed them down. Praise God! That boss of yours, who thinks he is going to fire you in the morning, is in for a big surprise. The government officials who have been refusing to give you legal papers are about to do so at last. Things are about to shift in your favor because God is about to do some amazing things in the camp of the enemy. Why? Because it's time for you to move forward, and nothing must be allowed to prevent that from happening. God Himself will take care of what hinders.

It is time for all of your business ventures to move forward. It's time for your ministry to move forward. It's time for your personal life to move forward.

It's time to move forward! No more delays!
It's time to move forward! No more delays!
It's time to move forward! No more delays!
It's time to move forward! No more delays!

Get that into your spirit, and let it move you from your complacency.

"Isaac Went Forward"

Genesis 26:13 records the fact that Isaac *"went forward."* He went forward, and you must go forward too.

Remember that *forward* speaks of position. Now, combining that with the past tense becomes very powerful. He did it. He *went forward*. And what was the result?

> *And the man waxed great, and went forward, and grew until he became very great: for he had possession of flocks, and possession of herds, and great store of servants: and the Philistines envied him.*   Genesis 26:13-14

Understanding the Seed, Part III

The Lord blessed Isaac for having obeyed Him and for having sowed in a time of famine (verse 12). The result was that Isaac *"waxed great,"* he *"went forward,"* and he continued to grow until *"he became very great."* To understand this fully, we need a grasp of the archaic English in which it was written.

When the Bible says, he "went forward," it is saying that he moved or went past his time. It was then that he *"became very great."*

If you will remember, in chapter 6 we looked at the word *success*. Isaac continued with greatness until he became very great. He went forward. He became successful in every way.

Now it's your time to move forward. From this day and this moment, refuse to take a single step backward. Refuse to sit and ponder what you should be doing. Move forward. If evangelism has been a problem for you, start testifying to your neighbors. Invite them to go to church with you. This grace is already upon you. Move forward in it.

All of your forward actions will soon yield good fruit. Therefore follow the Lord's instructions. Move forward.

"The Egyptians you have seen today you shall see them no more for ever." Pharaoh and his team are no problem for God, and they should not be a problem for you either. Let Him handle them. You just move forward.

Some wonder if they will ever preach again. I can say to them, "Move forward. You will preach many times in the days ahead. Your I-don't-know attitude has been killed and will be buried with the Pharaoh and the other Egyptians. You know now, so move forward."

You are the seed of God, and you will possess the gates of your enemies. A great and mighty revival has broken forth, and God is raising up more revivalists. Will you be one of them? Then, move forward.

Get ready to go. If there are things that have hindered you, deal with them quickly. You must move forward.

Unlike Anything in the Past

This current revival is unlike anything we have experienced in the past. Other revivals happened in one place and at a particular time. This revival will happen everywhere at once.

This revival will not be attributed to one person or a small group of people. People all over the world will be moving with the Lord in the days to come.

So this is a time for the seed, and that means we are due for a great harvest. What should you do? Go forward.

Rejoice, for your future will be far brighter than your yesterdays. Greater things are yet to come — the best. Let Pharaoh come, for we are ready for him.

Pharaoh is not your problem because he is behind you. Forget him and focus on what is ahead. What are our clear instructions for the immediate future? Move forward in them.

Amen!

Contact Page

You may contact Pastor Peter Kange in the following ways:

11214 Snowden Pond Road
Laurel, MD 20708

Email: soldout4one@gmail.com

Telephone: 301-859-4070 Ext 4

Contact Page

You may contact Lady Jane Lowder in the following ways:

Calvary Pentecostal Campground
11352 Heflin Lane
Ashland, VA 23005

Telephone: 804-798-7756

Email: Info@CalvaryCampground.org

Website: www.CalvaryCampground.org

CONTACT PAGE

You may contact Harold and Andrea McDougal in the following ways:

18896 Greenwell Springs Road
Greenwell Springs, LA 70739

Harold: hmcdougal@bellsouth.net
Andy: AndysMinistry@aol.com

Office: 225-262-1937
Home: 225-330-4492
Cell: 225-964-2274

www.ThePublishedWord.com

www.ingramcontent.com/pod-product-compliance
Lightning Source LLC
Chambersburg PA
CBHW032100090426
42743CB00007B/191